The Moose's Children:

A Memoir of Betrayal, Death and Survival

David M. Mokotoff

INFINITY
PUBLISHING

On the cover (left to right): Christine "Tina" Marie Ackerson, Bruce "Moose" Ackerson, and Bruce Allen "Bud" Ackerson, Jr., *New Jersey, circa 1958.*

Copyright © 2011 by David M. Mokotoff

ISBN 978-0-7414-6957-1 Paperback
ISBN 978-0-7414-6958-8 eBook

Printed in the United States of America

Published December 2011

INFINITY PUBLISHING
1094 New DeHaven Street, Suite 100
West Conshohocken, PA 19428-2713
Toll-free (877) BUY BOOK
Local Phone (610) 941-9999
Fax (610) 941-9959
Info@buybooksontheweb.com
www.buybooksontheweb.com

Table of Contents

Acknowledgements

This project would not have been possible without the help and advice of many people. The patience, love and support of my wife, Denise, and my three daughters, Rachel, Sarah and Emily were vital. The frank and honest interviews of the Ackerson sisters were likewise invaluable, and without them, this memoir would not have happened. Therefore I would like to extend my thanks, love, and gratitude to Pam Barden of Ft. Myers, Florida, Sue Callahan of Dunnellon, Florida, Jodi Lane of Pembroke Pines, Florida, Penny (Mary Kim) Weinger of Hollywood, Florida, Meighan Jenks of Alpharetta, Georgia, Janeen Tribou of St. Petersburg, Florida, and Bruce Allen "Bud" Ackerson, Jr. of La Crescent, Minnesota. I also thank Jeanice Bunday for her time and honesty in recounting her time with Robert, "Bobby," Ackerson, and Beth Morean for her help and feedback.

Fawn Germer, Kathy Murphy, Liz Burton, John Backus, Susan Reverby, and Colleen Weiss supplied critiquing and manuscript reviews tirelessly. Jayne Pupek, who died August 30, 2010, also assisted with a large part of the editing. My thoughts and prayers are with her and family—she was a gifted writer, poet, and teacher who never sought notoriety, although certainly deserved it.

During periods of family stress, friends and neighbors provided selfless support and generous time. In particular, I would like to recognize the Posey, Weiss, Nunnelly, and Neustadt families.

Jim Simons, Linda Fisher-Morgan, and Morgan Vasigh at Medical Publishing Group in St. Petersburg, Florida also provided great assistance and suggestions.

Erin Merryn for agreeing to write the foreword has been a beacon of light for those who have long suffered in secret the shame and indignation of rape, incest, and child abuse.

And finally to all of the wonderful people in the Al-Anon fellowship, and my Toltec friends, I could not have made it through this chapter in my life without you.

Introduction

This work describes a period in my life, and as such is non-fiction. However, as with all memoirs, my recalling and portrayal of events may be different from others who were present at the same time. I have tried to corroborate my telling of the Ackerson siblings' upbringing as much as possible from more than one of the sisters of my late wife, Christine (Tina) Marie Ackerson. Since Tina's father, Bruce, "Moose" Ackerson, and her brother, Robert Ackerson are deceased, their stories had to be assembled from my memory and other family members' recollection. Two of the brothers declined interviews. One brother asked that his name not be mentioned at all in the book and therefore is identified only as X. Just prior to publication he contacted me and stated that he had not been sexually abused. The perpetrator of the crimes, Victor Morgan, died on January 15, 2011. His widow, Helen Morgan, as of this writing is alive, but suffers with Alzheimer's dementia, and therefore was likewise not interviewed.

Foreword

Childhood sexual abuse is an epidemic. According to the National Children's Alliance one in four girls, and one in six boys, will be sexually abused before their eighteenth birthday. Sexual abuse has long-term effects, and healing is a lifelong process of therapy and challenges. Some of the more common problems seen in survivors of sexual abuse are eating disorders, self-injury, depression, suicide, promiscuity, addictions, and substance abuse. Without the proper therapy, the abused victim will stay stuck in the pain of the past, with all the problems that ensued.

The dilemma in our society is the failure to educate children at a young age to speak up if someone ever tries, or does, touch them. Because of the associated stigma and shame, many survivors do not break their silence until adulthood—long after the abuse has ended. Sexual predators have a way of not only threatening a child, or someone they love, to stay silent through violence, they also make a child feel as if the abuse is their fault. Children frequently carry this burden of guilt into adulthood, thinking they are responsible for what happened because they did not speak up and tell someone.

As a survivor of childhood rape and molestation from not one, but two people, I know what a survivor goes through long after the sexual abuse has ceased. Had someone empowered me as a child to use my voice and tell someone what was happening, I believe I would have told someone much sooner than I did. Instead, I kept my secrets locked away in a childhood diary, which I would later publish in my first book *Stolen Innocence*. I then completed my master's degree in social work, and published my second book, *Living for Today*, where I talk about my vision to pursue a law to educate children in public schools on sexual abuse through age appropriate curriculum. That law—Erin's Law, was signed by Governor Quinn in my home state of Illinois on February 14, 2011.

As I read *The Moose's Children*, I found myself stopping often to realize how the author must be a unique and strong person. A man who has experienced betrayal and heartache over and over again, does everything he can to help his alcoholic wife. Yet at the same time, he is still present to balance being a father to his three daughters, and the best heart doctor to his patients. What David Mokotoff endures in his marriage and family for more than a decade, is one many spouses would have walked away from early on. Rather he chooses to stand by his wife's side—almost to the very end.

As we say in our wedding vows,"in sickness and in health, and until death do us part." David Mokotoff held his vow much longer than most. Ultimately, he came to realize he needed to do what was in the best interest of his daughter Emily.

David Mokotoff did everything he could—he put his wife in the top rehab programs in the country and was remarkably supportive of her. The reader becomes a witness to her constant battle for sobriety. At times you witness her celebrating months of abstinence—even years. The fundamental issue is her unresolved abuse as a child, and the resulting alcoholism and addiction to shopping. The addictions grow and blossom out of the secrets from her childhood that her husband had no clue about until years after they are married. The night he learns that his wife has secrets she has been keeping about her stepfather, he responds in a way I hope every man or woman would do in a relationship. He simply asks her if she wanted to talk about it instead of changing the subject or denying its veracity. The confession then opens up chapters of her life that she has kept secret for decades. The repeated sexual abuse directs her to alcohol as a way of numbing the painful memories she will never be able to forget.

The Moose's Children describes how the aftermath of unresolved abuse as a child can affect not only the survivor, but also an entire family. *The Moose's Children* searches for answers of what happened to Tina, and her siblings, as children, as revealed through interviews with several of Tina's sisters. We discover what a monster her stepfather, Victor Morgan, really was as he sexually and physically abused his stepchildren for personal gratification. As a result, the common pattern of stigma and shame follows the survivors into adulthood. *The Moose's Children* is an assessment of how powerful sexual abuse can be on children's lives—from the threats that keep them silent into adulthood—to the challenges they must face at every life stage due to unresolved emotional injury. *The Moose's*

Children exposes the ripple effects to the husband, and daughter, of an alcoholic sexual abuse survivor.

Had Tina Mokotoff been empowered as a young child to break her silence, I believe we would hear her voice in this memoir. Instead, we must hear from those that loved her and did everything in their power, and beyond, to help her. My hope is that survivors, and family members of survivors, will read this and seek the help they, and their loved ones need, to deal with unhealed child abuse. Therapy begins by staring the past in the face and working through it—not numbing it with alcohol or other unhealthy addictions.

The stories each sibling shares will open your eyes to the horrific child abuse that goes on in our world. With an estimated 60 million survivors of sexual abuse in America, this is the story of some of those survivors and their loved ones. The powerful words spoken by David Mokotoff's daughter, Emily Mokotoff, and what she endured with her mother, will tug at your heart, and take you into the intimate world of living with an alcoholic parent. *The Moose's Children* is a powerful memoir that will keep you reading up until the very last sentence. I was in awe of how people can rise above betrayal more than once, and find the determination to help a spouse, protect a child, and seek answers to a monstrous family history.

Erin Merryn is a MSW, speaker, and author of *Stolen Innocence* and *Living for Today*.

Prologue

It was the ever present, sickly sweet orange blossom smell that Tina would most remember. Citrus trees surrounded the old clapboard house on Live Oak Road in Lakeland, Florida, and bees buzzed nonstop from one branch to another. The house's old air-conditioner groaned twenty-four hours a day, seven days a week during the long Florida summer, which seemed to stretch on forever. An ancient sprinkler system spewed rust-colored water from a shallow well onto the sidewalk, as it teased up irregular patches of St. Augustine grass mixed in with dollar-weed. The twelve hundred square foot home sheltered recently re-married Helen Ackerson and Victor Morgan, plus nine of her children from her first marriage, and her mother from New Jersey, Helen Isbister. It was her grandmother that Tina always remembered. When Helen and Vic were drinking, which was most of the time, it was grandma who cooked and cared for the children, and suffered the brunt of Vic's violent outbursts.

Tina's memory was splotchy, but never wavered.

"Vic shoved Vodka down my throat when I was only eight, and then he raped me when I was twelve."

She would repeat this story again and again to her sisters, and me many years later. Her emerald green eyes would lose their usual sparkle, and her dimples would disappear. I would note a hollow and vacant look on her face—neither angry nor sad—just a stark recounting of a horrible time. I didn't understand how anyone could confess to this and be so devoid of outward emotion.

"Get over here you little bitch!" Vic screamed.

"I'm going to whip your ass," he hollered in a drunken stupor. As her inebriated stepfather weaved through the house looking for her, Tina hid under the laundry in her closet. The sound of Vodka bottles shattering in the living room echoed in her head like canon fire. She covered her ears to block out the noise, and started humming.

"Oh please, Vic, leave the poor girl alone," her grandmother pleaded.

"Shut up!" he wailed at her. "She needs to show me some respect."

"But she's just a child," the old woman argued.

"She's just a child," he slurred, mocking his mother-in-law's defense. "Yeah, well, life's tough, isn't it? She needs to mind her elders who provide for her and do as she's told."

"You're drunk again. Leave her alone!"

"You tellin' me to leave her alone?" he puffed. And with that he lunged toward the elderly woman grabbing her arm. She kicked and yelled for her daughter to help her; however, Tina's mom, Helen, was passed out and snoring loudly in the bedroom.

"Get outta here you old bag!"

He was much taller, stronger, and younger than her. As the older woman was screaming, he tossed her outside into the cold December night air and locked the door. She banged relentlessly.

Tina covered her ears and began to hum again even louder, trying in vain to shut out the noises like so many times before. Finally, she couldn't listen to the commotion anymore.

"I'm going to get grandma," she whispered to her younger sister, Meighan, huddled next to her.

"No, please don't. I'm scared he'll hurt you."

"I don't care. I can't leave her out there cold and hungry all night." And with that she bolted out of the closet past the Christmas tree.

"There you are, you little shit," he yelled, "I'm goin' to kill you! You better do what I want."

She was younger, more agile and sober. Darting past him, he grabbed her leg, and she swung her arm, landing a right hook to his nose. Like a wounded tiger, this only seemed to enrage him more. He flung out for any part of her clothing, and tore her shirt. The tattered fabric fell to the floor and she screamed. Lunging, he grabbed both of her legs and pulled her to the bathroom. It was the only door lock that had not been disabled, and he quickly flipped the latch shut. Meighan banged helplessly on the thin door. Pummeling him powerlessly with closed fists, Tina screamed. She felt her panties being ripped off and then a calloused hand reaching between her thighs. She smelt the vodka in her in face and tried not to breathe. The last things she saw were the large veins on his temples pulsing.

Part One

~⚬~

The Moose's Children: A Memoir of Betrayal, Death and Survival

"Nobody abuses us more than we abuse ourselves"
                              −Don Miguel Ruiz

January 2004

Once again, I was left to pick up the pieces. Because she was dead, however, this time it seemed different—more final. Since our divorce nine months before, in March 2003, my youngest daughter Emily and I had progressively seen less and less of her, she being rarely sober. I had never stopped loving her, but ultimately found the disease too much to bear. I was functionally a single parent anyway, left to arrange nanny after nanny, while trying to hold down an exhaustive job as a cardiologist, complete with night and weekend call, and working sixty to eighty hours a week.

A few years before the final call came, Emily and I were visiting during Tina's latest episode of gastrointestinal bleeding, due to a cirrhotic liver and continued drinking. She was in delirium tremens (DT's) and didn't even know we were there. Emily sat on my lap outside her mother's door in the intensive care unit at Palms of Pasadena Hospital, a small 307 bed hospital in St. Petersburg, Florida; both of us staring at the yellow heartbeats racing across the dark screen. She was petite for ten years old, but full of energy and her long red curls caught all of the nurses' attention, as she bounced on my lap, fidgeting with strands of thin paper used to record patients' heart beats. Emily's mood became somber.

"I wish she would just die already," she said to me with little emotion or expression. We were both exhausted from this routine.

"I know that's how you feel sweetie, but that is up to God and your mom," I said, tempted to agree with her.

When Tina's end finally came, I was at another small hospital, St. Petersburg General, in the intensive care unit, seated at a nursing station, reviewing a patient's chart. The patient was a ninety-year-old woman who had had a heart attack and was probably not going to survive. Although she had a living will, the family was having a hard time letting the matriarch die and was torn about how much more they should do to keep her alive. My mobile phone rang, and I saw Tina's condo phone number flash on the caller ID. Momentarily frozen, I was unable to respond. She had stopped calling me weeks ago, and I had a premonition of terrible news.

As a nurse stared, expecting me to answer it, I finally hit the connect button. My mouth dry, I stared at the dull grey tiled floor before I spoke.

"Hello."

"Tina's dead," her mother, Helen told me, in between sobs.

"How? When?" My stomach tightened and I started to bite my cuticles, a habit which afflicted me when I had to deal with unpleasant tasks.

"Sue came over to visit her and found her dead on the couch."

I didn't ask for any more details, as her exact mode of death seemed unimportant to me at the time.

"The paramedics need the name of her doctor and..." Helen's voice faltered.

"I'll be right there. Tell them not to leave."

Quickly hitting the end button, I immediately called my office, explaining what had happened, and saying I could not finish work that day. Rising out of my chair, the same nurse approached me.

"Are you okay, Dr. Mokotoff?" I must have looked pale.

"Yes. I'll be fine. Thanks," I uttered, not wanting to go into any particulars. Even though the news was not unexpected, I felt stunned and saddened. I wasn't ready to share the news with my colleagues.

Driving the short seven-miles to her condo, my window down and A/C off, the cool January Florida air streamed in as I squinted out at a mix of high cirrus clouds and angled sunlight. January is one of the coolest months in West Central Florida. Most tourists envision eighty-degree weather and warm water, but the highs for this month are rarely above seventy, and the Gulf of Mexico water temperature often hovers around an uninviting sixty degrees. My only thought was how Emily would take the news. I remembered very little else, and upon arriving at the condo, I saw the EMS truck and local police cars outside. Two of her sisters, Sue and Janey, were holding each other weeping. After giving them both hugs, I noticed a scruffy looking thin figure in the background of the growing crowd.

"Who's he?" I asked

"Billy Barber. You know, her old boyfriend," Sue said subdued.

Wearing a long, worn black leather duster, boots, an open shirt, one-day-old beard, and long unkempt graying hair, he reminded me of the homeless men who held up signs begging for cash on the local street corners. Approaching, I did not reach out my hand. He smelled of cigarettes and stale beer, and had coke circles around his nose.

"I'm her ex-husband. What happened?"

Head partly bent, and with little eye contact, he hesitated a bit, then said, "She got sick last night and started to throw up blood. I asked her if she wanted to go to the hospital and she said no. I helped her to the bathroom, and then made her comfortable on the couch."

He stopped, made eye contact briefly, to see if I would judge his story believable.

"And then?"

"Then I left to go to the beach. I came back this morning and found her."

I knew he was lying.

The stench of death hit me as I entered the golf–fairway condo. Being a physician, I had long ago grown accustomed to it. However, the sight and smell of stale blood and vomitus was omnipresent. January 8, 2004. I remember every detail in the room like it was yesterday. Her mother, Helen, was standing off to the right in the kitchen sobbing, and two EMS technicians, in yellow jumpsuits, were taking notes on clipboards, and trying to look sympathetic. Specks of dust danced in the filtered late day winter sun, illuminating the living room where my ex-wife laid motionless on an overstuffed couch, a fine rivulet of dark blood hanging down one corner of her mouth. She was bloated, clothed in a sweats and a tee shirt, and I could neither move towards or away from her.

"This is your ex-wife, Tina Mokotoff, is that correct sir?" One of the paramedics asked.

"Sir?"

"I'm sorry," I said. "Yes."

"Are you her doctor?"

"No."

"Do you know who is? We need to speak with him about signing a death certificate," said a tall policeman in a starched navy uniform as his shoulder-mounted radio squawked. My eyes were glued to her corpse.

His voice was so matter-of-fact, and so final. Probably the same way I had been with dozens of families over the years when a loved one had died, and I was trying my best to act sympathetic. I gave the paramedics the name they wanted and after reaching him, I was told he would sign the death certificate, so there was no need for a coroner's autopsy.

"Do you have a funeral home yet?" asked one of the paramedics.

I nodded, having prepared myself for this exact moment. She had almost died nine years before of liver failure, after being diagnosed with cirrhosis due to a Hepatitis C infection and alcohol abuse. After two stays in rehab, she had been sober for about six years, and I had almost convinced myself again that we could have a long happy and loving life. Then came that awkward scene in Big Sky, Montana, in 2001, while we were on a family ski trip with friends.

For six years, when out to dinner, she would always refuse wine and turn her glass over. This time, however, her glass remained ominously upright, and when the waiter inquired, "Will you be having wine this evening ma'am?" she smiled and nodded, "Yes, just a little bit please."

I was stunned and horrified. I grabbed her arm softly to get her attention as she continued to chat with her girlfriends at the table. "What are you doing?" I whispered.

"Don't worry. It will be okay."

It wasn't okay, and for the next three years, she essentially never stopped drinking.

I had taken her to the University of Miami in 1995, and then the University Florida in 1996, where she had a liver biopsy. She was not judged to be a candidate for Interferon treatment, (a new anti-viral therapy for Hepatitis C), as her liver was too damaged. The liver specialist's enthusiasm for liver transplant was low as well, knowing that the virus often recurred and how difficult it was for alcoholics to stop drinking. I had seen enough alcoholics in my medical training die from internal bleeding or hepatic coma to know that if she kept drinking, the odds of her surviving more than a few years were slim.

"We're going to go ahead and cover her up now. Would you or the family like to spend any more time with her first?" A paramedic asked.

I declined, but glanced over at her shaking mother who nodded. She slowly walked toward the couch and in one effortless motion collapsed onto her daughter's dead body, heaving with wails and heavy sobs. Janey and Sue embraced and tried to console her. I needed to get outside—needed to get some air.

"Are you her next of kin?" another officer asked me. Rather than tell him the truth, I lied.

"Yes."

Pointing to Billy he said, "This gentleman would like to go back inside and collect some of his belongings, if that is okay with you."

No. It's not okay with me, I thought. Although I was under no illusion that he had killed her, I was certain that he had helped hasten her death. I had no hard evidence at this point, just a feeling.

"He also wanted you to know that if you look at her checkbook, there is a check for one hundred dollars made out to him that she had written yesterday."

"He can go inside for no more than thirty minutes, and only if accompanied by you or another officer," I answered full of suspicions.

He nodded and the pair walked inside. As I turned towards the front door, an ambulance gurney was leaving with a zipped-up black heavy plastic body bag. Although I had anticipated this inevitable moment for months, this seemed unreal, as if I wasn't really there. I told Helen I would take care of the funeral arrangements, giving her a polite hug. I needed badly to be alone inside this place where Tina had hidden away, and died slowly over the past year. I was still looking for answers that didn't exist.

My eyes followed the bloody trail of vomit from the couch to the half-bathroom where a fluffy sofa pillow had been placed next to the toilet. The large screen television was still blaring. I turned it off.

"I don't like to be alone. I need noise," she would often say to me.

For unknown reasons, I was drawn to the kitchen and started to open drawers. The one with the knives also contained a bunch of cut plastic straws, most likely used for snorting lines of coke.

The telephone message light was blinking and I picked it up the handset. I did not hesitate. Hitting the play message button I was greeted without having to enter a password. The prompts started immediately.

"First message, 1:32 a.m. today from 727-530-0415," said the non-descript female computer voice.

"Hey doll, I miss you already. Call me back. I'm at the beach."

"End of message. Press two to save and three to delete."

I hit two.

Next message, 2:45 a.m. today from the same number.

"Hey, it's me again. I just wanted to make sure you're all right—call me." Click. I pressed the number two again.

There were several more messages up to almost eight a.m., and the last one said, "Hey don't sleep in. You don't have room service there. Call me and I'll come over."

They were all from Billy Barber. He had obviously been up all night, probably hyped up on blow, and aware that he had left his girlfriend gravely ill. Scared, he most likely ran off. The more she didn't return the calls, the more he likely thought he might have to account to someone for her death. He couldn't take any chances since he already had a rap sheet, and her diamonds had mysteriously disappeared about one month ago. I was certain that he had hocked them to buy drugs.

"Hey, she was fine when I left. I wasn't there all night. See, here are all my phone messages," I imagined him telling the police.

I wanted to believe that he knew she was near death when he left the condo because I needed someone else to blame; someone other than her. But he left her there anyway. He left her there to die, drowning in her own blood and vomit. Then he called repeatedly to cover his own tracks and create a plausible alibi, just in case someone asked too many questions.

As I surveyed the condo, the walls were adorned with Emily's photographs. Emily in a big floppy Easter hat, Emily dancing and modeling—it was like Tina had created a shrine to our daughter. As I peaked inside her walk-in closet, there were unworn designer jeans and clothes, new tags still affixed. Upstairs, in her study, were bank statements strewn about with other important legal letters. Suddenly, I just needed to get outside—I felt as if I was suffocating.

Billy handed me the keys to the condo and her car, and I made a mental note to change the locks. I gave Helen, Sue and Janey one more final hug, and said I would be in touch soon.

Numbly, I drove the couple of miles back to my house, and as I approached the driveway, I steeled myself for the conversation I had long dreaded. Rebecca, Emily's latest live-in nanny, was there waiting in her teal Acura sedan, and as I got out, my face must have given everything away. Rebecca instinctively grabbed Emily's hand, and I bent my head a bit.

"She's dead."

Rebecca gasped and started to cry. Emily just stood at her side and stared off. We hugged and I knew what I had already known for years. I was all she had left in this world.

1985

—⟶~ᴜᴊᴜ~⟵—

"Dr. Mokotoff, could you smell this for me?" a voice said, diverting my attention from a patient's dense medical chart.

"What?" I said, glancing up at the wheeled beige cart, used to carry around medications to each patient's hospital room. A nurse stood next to it. I thought perhaps I had seen her before.

"It's Eldertonic. Have you ever tasted it?" she continued.

"No. What is it?"

"Dr. Patel orders it all of the time. I think it has elderberries and alcohol in it," she continued with a smile. Pouring a small amount of the purple liquid into a medicine cup, she held it under my nose.

"It smells hideous," I said, after sniffing the stuff. "It reminds me of cough syrup."

Saying nothing, she just looked at me in a demur fashion as I glanced back at her. She looked familiar.

"Do I know you?" I asked.

"Yes. Tina Ackerson," she replied. "I was a secretary on the med-surgery floor, and I used to take your orders off of charts. I just finished nursing school."

Yes, I had seen her before, but I had never noticed how beautiful she was before that moment. She had deep emerald green eyes, fluffy auburn hair, and two dimples beside attractive full lips, noticeable only when she smiled. I was frozen in place and felt myself staring at her face. I started to sweat and fumble for words. She could sense my embarrassment, and this seemed to only fuel her flirtation. She offered her hand, which I took, noticing her warm, soft skin.

"Yes, of course. Now I remember," I stammered, blushing. "What were you asking me?" I said trying to keep a professional demeanor. She showed me the cup of purple goo again.

"I asked if you'd ever tasted this?" she laughed.

"No."

Grasping the cup, I sniffed it cautiously, and then took a swallow.

"Not bad," I said. In truth, it tasted like cheap wine mixed with Robitussin.

"What is this stuff for anyway?"

"I think it's for old people, to stimulate their appetites."

"It's probably the alcohol more than anything else," I said.

She glanced at the cup, and then looked into my eyes. "You're probably right. Thanks for trying it. I guess I'll see you around."

"Yes, I guess so."

Striding away, I could not get her face out of my mind. Her coquettish smile kept flashing, and I found it hard to concentrate. Refocusing on patients and their medical charts and families, I did several consults, and ended up driving home with Tina's image burned in my mind.

My marriage had been in trouble for a long time. When we married, we were both twenty-one years old, and it was the summer before starting medical school. Barbara, my first wife, was an audiologist, (hearing specialist), working on her master's degree. Other than both being Jewish, we could not have been more different. She was prim and proper, full of social graces, and I naïve, inexperienced, and more laid back. Our sex life was lousy, medical school was hard, and one day I came home to the news no husband wants to hear.

"We need to talk," she said taking my hand and leading me to sit on an old Salvation Army purchased couch. We had only been married for two years.

"I've had an affair, and I'm sorry. It was a mistake, and I've broken it off. I've chosen to stay with you."

It was as if a grenade had exploded next to my ear. I felt sandbagged and was speechless, which was unusual for me. My mind wanted to grab facts and understand what she was saying.

"With who and why?" I asked.

"That's not important, I just think..."

"Not important?" I screamed at her. "Are you kidding? I've been working my butt off while you've been fucking someone else, and you think that's not important?"

She was boxed in, but showed little emotion.

"No. What I meant was who wasn't important, not why."

"Okay then. Why?"

She hesitated, twisting her lightly freckled hands together, and then it spilled out.

"Because you haven't satisfied me sexually," she said.

We were both virgins when we met in college, and in retrospect this wasn't too surprising. She further detailed how our love life had lacked intimacy. I don't remember the rest of the conversation, but I do remember saying to myself *someday, I will get even.* It was a silent mantra I would repeat in the coming years, and even though I didn't realize it then, this was the moment my marriage started to dissolve.

Several days after the medication cart episode, Tina was seated at the nursing station by a phone, taking report on a new admission from the emergency room. I pretended to be working on a chart, but could not take my eyes off of her. My stare wandered from her face down to her high and full breasts, beneath the white starched uniform. As she stood up to speak with another nurse, I could not help but admire the curves of her hips. I struggled to focus. She smiled at me as she sat back down, and I was suddenly speechless, my mind tormented. As she stood up to go into the medication room, I decided to take a chance.

The medication room was a small four by six foot closet, with one door that opened inwards. Medications, coffee, juice, milk, and patient snacks were kept there. As I walked in after her, she was bending over to grab something from the fridge. Her buttocks strained at the cotton uniform's constraints.

I felt my pulse race. My face became poker hot. She looked in my direction.

"Oh hi again. Can I help you?"

"I was just coming in for some coffee…I didn't know you were in here." We both knew I was lying.

"Here, let me get that for you," she said taking a white Styrofoam cup out of my hand. As she reached for the Bunn coffee maker pot with the other arm, her cleavage became even more revealing.

Sniffing the scalded glass carafe, her faced scrunched up as she said, "This is old, from last shift, why don't you let me make you a new pot?"

"Okay," I said. My mouth was parched.

My discomfort must have been all too visible.

"Are you okay?" she asked softly.

Without even thinking, I spewed it out.

"No. Not really."

As she approached me I could smell her perfume, gardenias or honeysuckle—I wasn't really sure. She took my hands in hers and asked, "Can I help?"

"I don't know. It's a really long story."

I didn't wait for her to respond and blurted out, "Would you like to go out for a drink sometime?"

A bit flustered, she replied, "Well I don't know. I have a boyfriend, and I can see that you're married," her eyes fixed on my wedding band.

"Actually separated," I said lying.

As our faces began to draw closer, we stared into each other's eyes, a gaze that could have burned a hole in granite. As we were about to embrace and kiss, the door swung open, hitting my back, and an embarrassed nursing student started to apologize. I was certain the emotional electricity was palpable in the small stuffy closet air.

"It's okay," I said to the student. "I was just leaving."

Embarrassed, I immediately left the floor, forgetting my still brewing cup of coffee.

A half-hour later, my name was paged overhead. The telephone operator gave me the number, and I immediately recognized it was the extension of Tina's floor. I dialed quickly. She answered after two rings.

"I would love to meet you for a drink," she said softly.

She gave me her home telephone number and I promised I would call her. As I hung up the phone, I could think of nothing else. My chest pounded and my pulse galloped. The adrenalin rush clouded my thinking, but all I could do was picture her freckled face, auburn hair, and full rounded body.

It was a typical Florida day in May—hot, humid, and steamy. I had never been to the South Pacific before, but imagined this must be what Guam felt like. Being outside for more than two minutes caused rivers of sweat to push through even the lightest clothing. Barbara and I sat outside of Greenstreet's, a popular waterside restaurant, in Indian Shores, perched on the Intracoastal Waterway. There was barely a breeze, but at least we were under an umbrella. As the intense Florida sun bore down, I stared off at the water as Donzi and Boston Whaler boats came and went. I was sipping a Molson beer in an iced mug. Large pieces of ice and beer-slush broke off from the glass and floated amidst the bubbles. Barbara sipped her ice tea. As we waited for our burgers to arrive, our lack of conversation was making me edgy.

"You live in one of the most beautiful areas of the country, and yet you seem so depressed," Barbara said to me. Never one to circle an issue, she then cut to the chase, "David, are you having an affair?"

"No," I said immediately, thinking to myself, but I sure would like to.

"Why did you bring me out here then?"

I didn't hesitate. "I need some time away—a separation—you know as a trial."

Her porcelain skin became red and her expression dour. She opted to play the guilt card.

"This is going to destroy the girls." She was referring to our two daughters, Rachel, eight, and Sarah, four.

"I'm not happy. I need time to sort things out. I don't know if it's me, you, or us."

She tried to protest, but knew that when my mind was made up, I almost never changed it. For the moment, she was beaten.

"All right, but promise me again that you're not seeing anyone."

"I promise."

Clancy's was not the kind of place where any of my friends, or hospital staff, would frequent. Near the fishing docks, it was a popular watering hole for shrimpers, fishermen, and crabbers. It smelled of smoke, and the worn cedar plank walls were adorned with black fishing nets and crab traps. Lifelike plastic models of tarpon, grouper, and sharks, hung from the wall, shiny glass eyes staring at the patrons.

As I entered, it took a few moments for my eyes to adjust. A bleached blond waitress asked me if I was alone.

"No. I need a table for two please."

"Sure thing, sweetie," she said popping her gum. Her high black skirt and fishnet stockings made her look like a hooker, but the pencil stuck over her ear, and worn sun drenched face, pegged her as blue-collar barmaid. Her nametag said Joni. As I sat down, she asked, "Can I get you anything to drink?"

"Sure. What kind of beer do you have?"

"Bottle or tap?"

"Tap."

"Bud, Bud Light, Pabst, Coors, and Killian Red."

"I'll take a Killian."

"Sure thing," she said with a dull and distant look.

Looking around the room, I congratulated myself on this choice for a rendezvous with Tina. No one I knew could ever possibly show up here. After a few minutes, Joni delivered my reddish-brown brew in a frosty mug. As I sipped my drink, a Phil Collins song bounced off the planked walls in the background.

Suddenly, a large splash of sunlight poured in through the door. I squinted again as the pupils of my eyes narrowed. Then I saw her, and I had to catch my breath. She seemed taller than I remembered. Auburn hair perched delicately upon her shoulders. She wore a diving orange cotton top and a brown ultra suede skirt that stopped a few inches above her knees. Mahogany sandals and red painted toenails completed the picture. As she looked around, I waved. She moved over to me and as I caught the scent of peaches, I felt a rush. Not knowing whether to extend my hand for a cordial shake, or be forward with a kiss on the cheek, she took the pressure off by leaning over and kissing me first. Her breasts touched my elbow. Thankful that it was dark, I turned my blushing face toward her and simply said, "Thank you."

Cocking her head to one side, she smiled and responded, "You're welcome."

Just as she sat down, Joni was over instantly, chomping on her wad of Bazooka again. "What would you like to drink, hon?"

"White wine, please."

"Sure thing, doll. It'll be right up."

"How did you find this place?" she asked.

I lied. "A random finger in the phonebook."

"Not likely anyone we know will see us."

"For sure."

"So, Dr. Mokotoff, may I call you David?"

"Yes, please."

Skipping the small talk she got down to business. "How long have you been married?"

"Fifteen years."

"Wow. You got hitched young."

"Yeah. Long story."

"I've got a lot of time." Her dimples expanded as she smiled.

I was about to respond when the wine was delivered along with a bowl of salted nuts and pretzels.

"You two want to see a menu?"

I looked at Tina for guidance, and she shook her head. "No thanks. I'm fine."

"I'm good too," I said. In truth, I had been hungry but suddenly lost my appetite. Joni quickly moved away, saying, "Okay then. I will check back with you in a little while in case ya'll change your minds."

"You were saying?" Tina asked as she sipped her tall sweating glass of Chablis.

I paused, not knowing where to go next.

"Do you love her?" she asked.

"You don't waste any time, do you?" I replied surprised at her directness.

"I'm sorry. It's just that I have never been married, and I have been in and out of relationships before. I don't want to become someone's mistress."

"I thought we were just having drinks," I retorted.

"Yes. Of course." Tina took another big swallow of wine. She backed off.

"I loved her at first. But after her affair, something in me just snapped."

"She cheated on you first?"

"Yes."

"Why did you stay with her?'

"I've asked myself that for years. I'm not sure. God, honor, and country maybe?" I said aiming to lighten my pain. Then I opted for the truth. "It was probably just fear."

"Fear of what?"

"Being alone." I stared at my beer and became quiet. She sensed that a raw nerve had been touched. Picking up on my vulnerability, she reached over and took my hand. Her warm soft skin felt like a glove and as she rubbed my knuckles with sympathy, I said nothing.

"I'm sorry for being so direct. It's not really any of my business," she said.

I was still nursing my beer as she drained the rest of her wine. I decided to switch from defense to offense.

"How about you? How long have you been with this guy?"

The Moose's Children: A Memoir of Betrayal, Death and Survival

"Five years. Scott and I were engaged once and he broke it off. We separated for a while, and then started dating again."

"Do you live together?"

"No. I won't do that again until I'm sure…"

"Sure of what?"

"A real commitment."

I wasn't really listening. I was just staring at her and she knew it. Fishing for more information, she started to dangle the hook.

"Scott and I just don't seem right for each other. He's always cheating on me. I deserve better."

"Then go out and get it. You're incredibly beautiful, young, and smart. You shouldn't have any trouble getting dates."

Now it was her turn to blush. "That is so nice, thank you."

We chatted for almost an hour about favorite foods, movies, and music and discovered we had a lot in common. We both liked to cook Italian food, and listen to blues and jazz. After I finished my second beer, and she her third glass of wine, I motioned Joni for a check. I left her thirty bucks, which included a big tip. "Ready?" I asked.

"Yes."

My head was spinning now, hammered on just two beers and lust. She however, seemed hardly fazed.

"Where is your car?" I asked, as we exited into the heavy air. The sun was setting behind swirls of red and orange clouds. Thunder rolled in the distance.

"Over there." She pointed to an old maroon colored Toyota and I walked her to it. Pulling keys out of her purse, she opened the door, tossing in both on the front seat. Turning towards me, before I realized what was happening, she took my face in both hands, and planted a luscious full kiss. Feeling her tongue exploring my mouth, I responded in kind, and felt hot. As her leg curled around mine, my arm reached around to the small of her back, and I drew her in closely. Bodies pressing, I could feel myself flush and stiffen. She pushed me away.

"That was very nice," I said feeling quite awkward.

She just smiled and said, "You haven't seen anything yet, buddy."

And like that she was gone.

I rented a fully furnished high-rise apartment on Redington Beach, overlooking the Gulf of Mexico. On my last night at home, I chose to

16

sleep on the couch downstairs. I entered the master bedroom to access the bathroom. Barbara was sitting on the bed rubbing her eyes with a tissue.

"We better tell the kids soon," I said.

"If you have the time," she said tightening the muscles in her jaw.

Ignoring her cynicism, I went into the bathroom, peeled off my old surgical scrub clothes, and entered a steaming hot shower, where I stayed in longer than usual. As the hot water pounded my body, I stared down to my belly, which had the start of a small bulge. Stepping out onto the rug, I surrounded myself with a large towel and found her perched on top of the toilet seat, still sniffling.

"Don't you have anything to say to me?" she asked.

I paused, knowing better than to say what was really on my mind. *If you hadn't cheated on me years ago, we wouldn't be in this fix today. Or you stifle me with your rules and phony social graces.* Instead, I opted for diplomacy.

"I'm sorry things have worked out this way. Let's just do what's right for the kids."

"You know it's not what I want. I want my friend and companion back again. The girls need a father too. You are working so many hours, I'm tired of being a single parent." She paused. "Do you still love me?"

Perhaps that might have been a good time to lie. However, I opted for the truth finally.

"No."

"Then I guess there's little more to discuss really. Why have you stayed married to me for so long then? That wasn't fair."

Standing very erect, arms crossed at the chest, she glared at me like a teacher about to tongue lash an errant student. She started to shake and then the iciness began to thaw. Small tears began to stream from the corner of each eye.

"I wasn't the one who cheated," I blurted.

"I thought we had worked that out a long time ago in therapy."

"Apparently not."

"How would I have known?" she sobbed. "You never talk to me about what you're feeling."

"Why bother? You think that you're always right. You know—the perfect wife, the perfect mother, just not the perfect lover."

That jab caused even more sobbing, but I could not even bring myself to hug or console her. Finally, I felt vindicated. She sat in a heap, mascara and makeup slowly dripping down her cheeks, and her chest heaving. Slowly she rose and collected herself, grabbed a terry-cloth bathrobe and descended the stairs.

I towel dried my hair, and tossed the large plush ivory wrap over the side of our deep Jacuzzi spa bath, an action I knew she detested. Naked, I quickly walked into my closet and put on clean blue surgical scrubs. As I stared at my clothes wondering when I would have the time to pack and move, my pager went off. I read the few words scrolled across the green screen—I needed to call the emergency room about an ill patient. Picking up the phone by the bed, I dialed the ER's number and was informed about a patient having a heart attack. I fled out the front door without saying good-bye to her.

She most often wanted to talk everything to death, but later that night Barbara was silent. As promised, we sat the two girls on the couch and I did most of the talking. My wife just sat still, like a statue, playing the innocent victim role. The dark room, with a built in mahogany entertainment center, and real wood fireplace, felt cold and empty.

"Mommy and Daddy still love you. We just don't love each other anymore," I explained.

"Why not?" Rachel, our oldest daughter asked, choking back tears.

"I don't know," I said.

Sarah, our youngest, just sobbed and gripped her sister's hand.

Barbara said nothing, letting me do all the talking—twisting from a noose. If there was going to be a villain in the girls' eyes, it certainly wasn't going to be her. In the end, this was all my idea, wasn't it? I on the other hand felt like I was being hung out to dry.

As warm tears poured from the youngsters' eyes, I continued to try and explain the inexplicable.

Setting the Hook

Most people want to believe that when we fall in love it is for the purest of reasons. This isn't always the case. Often lust comes before love, which was true of Tina and mine's relationship. The lust blinded me to her flaws or possible motivations for wanting us to date.

Several weeks after our rendezvous at Clancy's, I learned a bit more about why Tina decided to go out with me. We were talking on the phone one evening as I stared out at another luminescent sunset over the Gulf of Mexico.

"You have a boyfriend who is also your ex-fiancé. Why did you decide to go out with me?" I asked.

There was a brief hesitation on the phone and then she said, "At first, I thought it was a bad idea. But then I spoke with my mom, and she encouraged me to do it."

Instead of pressing for more information, I simply said, "Oh."

I had known her mother, Helen Morgan, for years. She was the medical secretary in the Cardio-Thoracic Surgical Unit at Northside Hospital. Short and a bit plump, she was a friendly woman who seemed to be chatting gossip when she wasn't taking physicians' orders from the medical charts. She was always kind and friendly towards me. Only later would I discover a darker side.

"What about Scott?" I asked her on the phone—referring to her boyfriend.

"I think turnaround is fair play. He's always been cheating on me."

So much for taking the moral high ground I thought. She wants to cheat on her boyfriend, and I'm about to cheat on my estranged wife.

"When can I see you again?" I asked.

"I am off this Thursday."

"Perfect. Why don't you come over to my condo around seven and I will cook dinner?"

"Really?" she answered. "Can I bring anything?"

"Just your beautiful self."

She wasn't just dangling a hook for me—I was more than eager to swallow the bait, hook, sinker, and the whole fishing line.

After work, I walked down a Publix grocery isle, picking out pre-made garlic bread, fixings for a salad, and ingredients for Veal Parmesan. Having spent a college summer interning under a Culinary Institute of America chef at a summer camp before ultimately going to college, I was more than a decent cook.

Entering the condo, I grabbed some ice water, turned on a Grover Washington, Jr. CD and jumped into the shower. After splashing on some cologne, I slipped on some sandals, Kaki pants, and a Tommy Bahama tropical shirt. Gazing out of the bedroom window at the setting sun, I inhaled the humid salt breeze and felt the air on my face. Taking in several deep breaths, I listened to the gently pounding surf, seagulls screeching, and the tree frogs who were just beginning to groan and croak. While Grover's soulful saxophone played "Winelight," I assembled the salad, placed the foil-wrapped bread in the oven, and started to prepare the thin veal cutlets by dipping them in egg wash and then Italian breadcrumbs. Losing track of the time, I jumped when the doorbell rang.

As I opened the door, the late day sun bounced off her hair. There were no handshakes today. She leaned forward and gave me a full wet kiss.

"Welcome. Please come in," I stammered.

She walked inside and as she gazed around her face beamed.

"Oh, this is so beautiful," she said gazing out the floor to ceiling picture window as the sun set over the water, producing multicolored ribbons of clouds.

"Drink?" I asked.

"Sure," she said, and extended me a chilled, but sweating bottle of white wine.

Taking the amber colored container from her hand, I reached for two glasses. Uncorking the bottle I poured the fruity liquid into the wineglasses. I could not take my eyes off her. Her outfit was a copper colored V-neck blouse and a white flowered sarong, draped lazily over her hips, tied on the side. The bottom was slanted on one leg, revealing a sliver of thigh. She took my perspiring hand and we walked with glasses over to the window.

"I cannot believe how gorgeous this is and I've lived here my whole life. Have you been here long?"

"No. Less than one week."

Sitting quietly on the couch, I sipped my wine, while she finished hers quickly, and then reached for a refill.

"Hungry?" I asked.

"Starving," she answered, "How about you?"

"Famished."

"Need some help in the kitchen?"

"Perhaps. Do you cook?"

"I love to," she answered.

"I can't believe it. Me too."

"That's unusual. I haven't met too many men who like to cook, other than of course barbeque."

"Well, you're looking at one now." We both laughed.

She swirled the butter and olive oil in a pan as I reached into the fridge for the marinara sauce. She sautéed the veal and then drained it on paper towels, and I placed the gently browned cutlets in a glass pan, covered it with sauce, and then added Mozzarella and freshly ground Parmesan cheese. I cranked up the oven temperature a bit, took out the bread, and placed the meat in the center.

"Why don't we have our salads while this is cooking?" I asked.

"Sounds great," she said. "Is this a Grover Washington, Jr. CD?" she asked.

"Yes. Do you like him?"

"I love him," she answered.

The sky continued to paint a pastel palette of colors. We made small talk again about interests in music and movies. I could not stop staring at her.

The timer sounded in the kitchen and I started to get up.

"Why don't you let me get it?" she offered.

"Okay," I relented.

She found the plates and dished out the veal along side some pasta. As we ate, our appetites for food quickly faded. Drinking half of the bottle of chardonnay, I was dizzy. This was far more than I usually consumed. She however seemed unfazed. As with her three drinks at Clancy's, I missed yet another warning sign. We both cleared the dishes to the sink in silence. As she washed them, I moved behind her. Wrapping my arms around her waist, I gently kissed her neck. Inhaling her perfume, I was even more intoxicated by the smell. My head was pounding—arousal coupled with too much alcohol. She hummed a bit, dropped a plate in the sink, and turned towards me slowly. Her hands encircled my waist, and we drew closer. I felt her velvety skin melt into mine.

As our mouths met, I could feel her breasts against my chest. We exchanged a long kiss and she let out a soft moan. Taking her hand, I led her to the sofa in the living room. She reclined on the plush material, grabbed my shirt, and drew me down. I could feel the gentle curves below, and as her hips started to rotate slowly, I could feel my arousal building. My mouth moved from her mouth to the nape of her neck and then to the valley between her breasts.

"I want to make love to you," I whispered in her ear.

Saying nothing, she sat up, removing her blouse and sarong slowly. Her breasts bulged out of her bra, and I started to tear open my shirt. As I was removing it, she was already unzipping my pants. My under shorts could barely contain the swelling any longer. As I kissed her again, I wasn't that drunk to forget a practical question.

"Do I need a condom?"

"I'm on the pill."

"Would you like to move to the bedroom?" I asked.

She nodded.

Leaving behind a trail of discarded clothes, we stumbled to the bed. She collapsed on her back and I nearly dove on top of her. I fumbled with her front clasp bra until she giggled and brushed my hand away to unlock it. I removed my shorts as she tossed her panties onto the floor. We exchanged a very long and deep kiss as she reached down and gave me a long squeeze.

As I slid inside of her we moved in unison, and it seemed like I came quickly. We cleaned up, and lying on my back, her mouth descending over my groin and I became quite erect again. This time she mounted me and we made love for what seemed like an hour. Exhausted and sweaty, we collapsed into a unified heap of limbs and entwined sheets. As I played with her hair, I mumbled, "That is the best sex I have ever had." She said nothing, but just smiled. As she sashayed away from the bed naked, clothes in tow, I watched her travel out to my spare bathroom. Moments later she emerged, clothed and sporting new lipstick.

"I would love to see you again sometime," I said as we kissed and hugged.

She was playing coy. "We'll see."

"I'm bringing the girls over to your condo this weekend," Barbara said on the phone to me the next day. It was Friday and my weekend to have Rachel and Sarah over. "Do you mind if I come in and see the place?"

Taken aback, I quickly answered, "Sure," without even thinking. I would regret it.

After work, I made sure to tidy up a bit, but forgot to look in the guest bathroom.

Our girls quickly donned their swimsuits and raced out to the beach.

On their way out, I shouted, "No going into the water until I'm out there. Okay?"

They both nodded and raced out to the elevator that would take them to the ground floor and the beach.

I had heard of too many water tragedies since moving to Florida, and Barbara and I had given them both swimming lessons at a young age. They were excellent swimmers. I was just playing the cautious parent.

"May I use your bathroom?" Barbara asked.

"Of course," I said. Without warning there was a knot in my stomach. I had not inspected the bathroom since Tina had left the night before. It wasn't long before Barbara came out red-faced and I knew there was trouble.

"Could you come in here for a minute?" she asked in a firm and demanding voice. It wasn't a request as much as an order.

As I walked in, I could not help but look at the mirror. I felt like I had been punched in the gut by a hammer. The words were emblazoned on the mirror in fire engine red lipstick.

"I had a great time this evening. Hope to see you again soon." The outline of a heart and Tina's signature followed.

"So you're not having an affair, huh? Then who is this?"

Choosing my words with caution, I said, "I wasn't lying to you when I said I wasn't having an affair. That was a month ago."

"Somehow I don't believe you. Who is she?"

"A friend."

"You're sleeping with her aren't you?" she pressed.

"I don't want to discuss this right now."

Usually composed, she was now shaking and her hands began to tremble.

"I can't believe you would do this! Do you hate me that much?" Her voice was shrill.

"No. I don't hate you. I just don't love you anymore."

And with that she threw her hands up, turned quickly and reached for the front door. She couldn't leave however without one last stab.

"Does she have big tits?"

I stared stone-faced as she roared out, the door slamming. Any illusion I had that this would be an amicable divorce left in the wind with her. Hanging my head, my pulse still racing, I went to the fridge and pulled out a Red Stripe beer. After cleaning the message off of the mirror, I pulled on some swim trunks, went down the elevator to the beach, and tried to pretend everything was normal as I played in the waves with my daughters. As I dove under Sarah's legs and rose above the surface, I grabbed her ankles as she balanced on top of my shoulders. We both knew the drill and said in unison, "One, two, and three!"

She pitched forward and dove into the teal-colored water. Coming up squealing, she yelled, "Again."

As we played this game a dozen more times, Rachel scampered back to the beach. She had never been a big fan of the ocean and sand, finding the gooey bottom and things that moved under toes frightening. Finally, Sarah and I swam back to shore.

"Who wants Pizza and Ice Cream?" I asked.

"I do, I do," they both yelled.

We went back to the condo to shower and dress. I pretended everything was okay.

"A penny for your thoughts," Tina asked on Monday morning as I sat pouring over a patient's medical chart.

"It's a long story," I said. "Besides there are ears all over the hospital, you know."

She nodded.

"Call me later, okay?" she said.

I nodded. After finally finishing work about eight o'clock in the evening, I picked up some Thai takeout, went home, and sat with my feet propped up on a wicker footstool, staring out at the dark waters.

A few lights on the beach shimmered, marking the nesting places of endangered sea turtles. I washed down my noodles with a Thai beer and ice water and dialed her number.

"Barbara knows about you," I said.

"Uh-oh. How?"

"She was dropping my kids off last Friday and used the guest bathroom. She saw your message."

"I'm so sorry," she said. "I had no idea she would be coming over to your place. You should have warned me."

"I didn't know either."

"Let me make it up to you okay? Are you on call tomorrow night?"

"No. I'm not on call for two more nights. What did you have in mind?"

"I'll make dinner at my house. How about seven again?"

"Okay. What shall I bring?"

"Just some wine and an appetite."

The next night I went home quickly to shower. She had given me directions, and it turned out her place wasn't far from the hospital. I picked up a bottle of California Chardonnay and some flowers. Her small rented home sat back from the road a bit, and was a typical Florida 1950's home—one level, metal awning carport, screened porch, and crushed oyster shell driveway. Her beat up maroon Toyota sat in the driveway. After ringing the doorbell and extending the flowers and wine, we kissed and she asked me inside.

"Rough weekend, huh?" She asked.

"Yes," I said, feeling subdued.

"Let me pour you a glass of wine and you can relax while I make dinner."

"What's on the menu?"

"Shrimp and pasta prima vera. You're not allergic are you? I'm sorry, I forgot to ask."

"No, not at all. I love shrimp."

Her small kitchen adjoined the family room where some old couches and a small television and stereo were located. The smells wafting through the air were not all fishy—rather the smell of the sea, indicating fresh seafood. After placing the flowers in a pitcher, she pulled the cork on the bottle and brought me a chilled glass. Her attire was simple—a flowered rayon blouse, simple white skirt and sandals. Her auburn hair was still wet, but fluffy from a recent shower.

"Are you sure I can't help?" I asked.

"Oh all right. If you insist, you can set the table. Come on in and I will show you where everything is located."

We talked about our day at work and kept avoiding the Barbara issue. As we sat down to eat our pasta and salads, she finally broke the ice.

"I'm sorry about leaving that message on your mirror. I didn't expect your wife to show up though."

"I know. It's not your fault. She would have found out sooner or later I suppose," I said, trying not to dwell on the issue.

"You still seem pretty upset," she said in between forkfuls of shrimp.

I sipped my wine and thought for a moment.

"This is really hard for me. Even though I don't love her anymore, I still feel like what I'm doing is awful." I was staring down at my plate, withdrawn and quiet. Without saying anything, she got up and stood behind my chair and started to rub my shoulders. It felt good. The smooth jazz station on the stereo was playing an Anita Baker song, and I reached up to grab her hand. Rising out of my chair, I encircled her waist, and we began to share a long kiss and embrace. As I lead her to the couch and started to reach under her blouse, she pulled away from me.

"What's wrong?" I asked.

Biting her lip, she said, "We can't have sex tonight."

"Are you bleeding?" I asked.

"No."

"Then what's wrong?"

She paused a long time with a pained and uncomfortable expression on her face. It took a few moments, but the truth spilled out.

"I should have told you this last week, but I have herpes."

Stunned, I backed away from her on the couch as if she had just told me she had leprosy.

"Come again?" I asked as my face warmed. I could feel my blood pressure rise.

"I got it from Scott. I feel unclean and dirty, and terribly ashamed.

I watch myself very carefully, and I swear I didn't have anything active last week when we were together. When I get upset, I start to feel numb and tingly in my back and leg, and then the outbreak starts. I only noticed it today. I don't think you can get it unless it's active."

"That wasn't fair of you not to tell me this, and besides it wasn't just your decision to make. Why didn't you tell me?"

She swallowed some wine and said, "Because I was afraid you wouldn't want me."

Confused and flustered, I got up and just walked out the door. The trip home seemed very long. I listened to a talk radio show on the AM dial for distraction, as my thoughts turned dark and angry.

I was in my office the next day when a certified letter arrived, and my secretary signed for it. It was from the Law Office of Leslie Franklin, my wife's marital attorney. Although, I was the one who had decided to file for divorce, I assumed that this would be his response to my recent filing. My mouth went dry as I read the details of the letter. Reading the legal jargon, I quickly got bogged down in words that made no sense to me like "marital residence," "irretrievably broken," and "loss of consortium." What got my attention however, were the dollar figures that flew off the pages attacking my eyes and mind.

"$4,000 per month in permanent alimony."

"$5,000 per month in child support."

"One-half of his IRA and pension plan."

"One-half of the value of the medical practice, to be determined later by a forensic accountant to be chosen by the wife."

"All of the wife's legal and accounting costs."

"The wife to retain control of the marital home and all of its contents."

It just got worse and worse. Clammy and perspiring, I felt nauseous, and without thinking, I just reacted. Picking up the phone, I called Barbara at home.

"Hello," she answered.

"I just read your attorney's letter. This is outrageous." I yelled.

"David," she said in her saccharin-sweet and patronizing voice. "Both of us know this marriage is over. The sooner we get on with the messy details, the better off the girls will be."

"That may be," I argued. "But the money you are asking for is absurd. That is far more than one half of my income and net worth!"

"You seem to forget that it was you who walked out on your family, and there is now three of us to support and only one of you. Besides, I helped get you through medical school and went through all of those lean years before you made a decent income. We're separated now, so this shouldn't come as a surprise to you."

Speechless, I decided it was best to end the conversation immediately. "I can assure you that I'm not abandoning my kids. However, I'll be damned if I'll let you walk away with that much money." And with that I slammed the receiver down onto the phone so hard that a pencil holder became airborne.

I sat fuming and played the conversation over and over again in my head. I felt alone and isolated. I was giving up a lot by walking away from my wife of fifteen years and now was involved with a nurse who had an STD, and hadn't been honest with me about it. I didn't think things could get any worse. I was wrong.

Obsession

I fooled myself into thinking that Tina's forced confession about her STD was a minor indiscretion. My need to see her was like a drug that I was powerless to stop using. I was willing to ignore any warning signs or half-truths, so long as I could continue to see her, speak to her on the phone, and make love in a way more passionate and exciting than I had ever experienced. I rationalized my prurient behavior with thoughts like: *I have a right to be happy and in love; She (meaning Barbara) cheated on me first; When you're thirsty in the middle of a desert, you don't stop to ask about the character of someone offering you water.*

I watched my groin with detached clinical interest over the ensuing weeks but saw no signs of genital herpes. It was not long before lust trumped logic or caution, and after she gave me the "all-clear" we began having sex again.

"What's the most unusual place you've made love?" I asked her one night, as we lay entangled in each other's arms in my bed, watching a full moon reflect shimmering gray light off of the gulf waters.

Rising on one elbow, with head cocked to one side, she appeared to think for a moment. My new pearl-white satin sheets rested underneath her breasts as she spoke.

"I would have to say in a bathroom aboard a 747 jet between LA and Hawaii."

"Really?" I asked, intrigued. "I thought that stuff only occurred in movies. Who did you go to Hawaii with and when?"

She hesitated a moment, as if unsure she wanted to tell me everything at once. Her face went from a smile to serious, and I noticed a blush beneath her freckles.

"Just after high school, in 1974, my best friend Chris and I hitched out to California. That's where we met Gary Hines."

Gary had an unusual occupation—he robbed banks. Over the next hour, I listened to her describe in vivid details how she drove getaway cars, and one time had a pistol cocked and held to her head. They would launder the stolen money through Reno and Lake Tahoe casinos by buying and selling chips to exchange later for "clean bills." Gary and his accomplices, including Tina, were finally caught. Both were sent to prison, where Tina claimed she was in a cell with Lynette, "Squeaky" Fomme, a former Charles Manson family member, remembered for an attempted assassination of President Gerald Ford.

"She was just weird," Tina said.

"So how long were you in jail?" I asked.

"Only a couple of weeks. My dad flew out to California, hired an attorney and got me back to Florida."

"So you have a felony criminal record?" I asked.

"No. My dad hired a really good lawyer and the record was expunged."

"So where's Gary now?"

"Still in prison—San Quentin, I think."

"You really had a wild time out there, huh?" I asked. (Her story seemed so improbable that I never fully believed it until it was later corroborated by her friend Chris DeRobertis.)

"Oh yeah, we did it all," she said without further elaboration.

I had the sense that she was baring her soul more than bragging. I needed to feel that she had some sense of morality and hoped she had remorse about this period in life. As a doctor whose job it was to elicit a detailed history from my patients, I pressed on.

"By doing it all, did you mean drugs?" I asked.

"Only a few times. But I never shot up anything." She hesitated for a moment. This would later turn out to be a "not exactly" moment.

"What else?"

"He made me participate in sex with him and another girl. I didn't like it," she said, before I could even ask.

By now, I didn't want to hear anymore. The whole sex trio thing had turned me on and she sensed my arousal. Her head snuggled under my chin, and in a few moments she had mounted me again for another round of lovemaking.

We would later have sex in some unusual places as well—under some Oleanders near the eighteenth green of a local golf course late at night and while swimming in the warm summer waters of the Gulf of Mexico. The riskier the environment, the greater the turn-on was for both of us.

It was late September 1987 and still as hot as July. Everyday was ninety plus degrees with humidity so high, it could squeeze sweat from a corpse. The only respite was the daily thunderstorms, which cooled things off a bit. I was living now in a three-bedroom condo in the Bardmoor area, near a golf course in mid-Pinellas County. One evening after a brief, but drenching thunderstorm, I waited for Tina to come over, so we could go out for dinner. As had now become my custom, I kept a half-gallon jug of white wine in the refrigerator. After we swam and showered together, she poured herself a tall glass. I drank water, and hardly noticed that she would have two or three of these, followed by a bottle shared with me at dinner. She did not seem drunk—just relaxed.

Waiting for our dinner, she appeared to have something on her mind. Finally, she spoke.

"My sister Sue's second son, Brian, was just born. He has spina bifida. They say if they don't operate in the next few months, he may never walk normally. I feel so bad for her." Spina bifida is a birth defect that involves the incomplete development of the spinal cord or its coverings. Because of the abnormal development of and damage to the spinal cord, a child with the most severe form typically has some paralysis.

"I'm sorry to hear that. Is there something you would like to do to help?"

"They have good insurance, and I can probably drive up to Gainesville, where they are going to operate, to be with them."

"Sounds like a good idea. How about donating blood?"

She became silent, and a small tear appeared in the corner of her eye.

"I can't."

"Why not?"

"Because the last time I tried to give blood, they said my liver tests were abnormal."

"So you have hepatitis?" I asked, stunned.

"Yes. They don't know what kind, but it is not A or B. I don't think it's contagious."

My face warmed. I felt sucker punched again.

"You don't think it is contagious? You're not a doctor. Jesus Christ, why didn't you tell me this before we had sex?"

31

"Because I was scared that you wouldn't want me." There it was again—the same excuse as with the herpes. *Strike two*, I thought.

I was speechless. Sitting there and watching her cry, I could not punish her anymore. However, the following day, I stopped at a medical lab and had a hepatitis and HIV test done—both were negative.

During the subsequent throes of my separation and divorce, I became so depressed that I decided to see a therapist. Upon his advice, I tried dating other women—even slept with a few. But I could never remove Tina's place in my soul. She ran off on a ski trip with another guy to Aspen, Colorado and I was devastated. Pleading with her on the phone one morning, I promised her a true commitment when she returned. I asked her to move in with me and she said no. She did not want to make the same mistake she had made with Scott, her ex-fiancé.

"I need more of a commitment than that," she told me.

"I promise you I will—please just wait until my divorce is final."

We agreed to date other people. She continued to work full-time at the hospital and we would cross paths often at work. When we did, the flames of lust and desire were always reignited.

I spent more time with my daughters and we shared good memories like movies, dinners, and trips to amusement parks. I was careful not to introduce them to any women whom I might be dating.

Still without a divorce agreement, I was spending money on accountants and attorneys as fast I made it. Barbara's attorney was bleeding me dry. That is the deliberate strategy—so you'll really get into a favorable negotiating mood—anything to stop the financial hemorrhaging. During the grueling fifteen months of negotiations, Tina was my lifeline and refuge. Before it was all over, I had spent $100,000 on attorneys and accountants for both of us. That's a lot of money today, and was even more in 1986.

My mind was distracted, and my work was being adversely affected as well. Two errors in judgment cost me two malpractice lawsuits while I was also going through the divorce process. I started to dread giving depositions and became even more depressed when I began to recognize the same court reporters.

Practically living together now at my condo, I felt it was finally time for Tina to meet my daughters. One night at Chuck E. Cheese,

I told them I had a surprise for them. At first, they thought it would be gifts. I introduced her as a "friend" and they looked at her with scrutinizing and suspicious eyes. However, she got down on their level shooting basketball hoops, and soon everyone was laughing and having a good time.

The next morning I got relatively good news. My medical malpractice insurance company had settled both cases without any admission of guilt. I felt some weight lifting from my shoulders.

The trauma of the divorce and the two malpractice suits prompted me to reflect about how little time I had made for my friends and family. I remembered a cardiology fellowship professor who had told the graduating class, "No one goes to the grave wishing they had spent more time at the office." Therefore, I committed myself to making more time for things other than work. I had a partner, Dr. David Kohl, who had joined me in 1985, and we were soon looking for a third doctor as well to handle our increasingly busy and successful practice.

Finally, in March 1988, my divorce was final. I felt as if a very large stone had been removed from my shoe. I was, however emotionally, physically, and financially drained.

After six months of relative quiet, I convinced myself that I had at last met the woman of my dreams. Tina was fun, loving towards my daughters, intelligent, and great in bed. Moreover, we both enjoyed gourmet cooking and dinners became a time of loving creation. Fine wines became increasingly frequent with dinners. Fetzer Chardonnay was replaced with Far Niente; Gallo Cabarenet Sauvignon with Jordan Reserve. We went to wine tastings almost every month and drank more than we should. I made sure to have another doctor take my call on these special evenings not wanting to risk doing a cardiac procedure while inebriated. At times I may have driven with a higher blood alcohol level than was safe. We made scuba diving trips to Key West and had a memorable ski vacation in Colorado. Suddenly the one-year anniversary of my divorce was looming. My practice was thriving, and I paid off my last legal bills.

After a special dinner of fresh summer spring rolls, grouper with mango salsa, and confetti rice, we opened a bottle of our favorite French Champagne, Perrier-Jouet. As I poured her glass in the kitchen, I dropped a 1.5-karat Marquis diamond ring inside and prayed she wouldn't swallow it.

"To our lives together," I said, raising my crystal fluted glass high.

As she held up her glass, she suddenly saw the ring and gasped. "Oh, my God!"

I went down on one knee. "Tina, will you marry me?"

She did not hesitate. "Yes."

We set a wedding date for October 22, 1989.

Moose

The first time I met Bruce Ackerson was at his home in Hollywood, Florida. Tina and I were engaged, and she tried to warn me about him in advance. "I love my dad, but he can be overbearing. He's also doesn't like gays, lesbians, or black people."

"Great," I said. "What about Jews?"

"No. I think he's okay with them."

"That's good, since most of his neighbors are probably Jewish," I responded, not to mention me as well.

"Any other phobias I need to be aware of?"

She thought for a moment and then said, "Oh yeah…he thinks there are too many Mexicans and Cubans moving into South Florida."

I must have rolled my eyes a bit, and she caught the unflattering image I was already creating in my precognition. "But promise me you won't judge him because of his prejudices," she pleaded.

The answer was easy because I loved her. "Yes, dear."

"Does he ever come up here to St. Pete to visit?" I asked, dreading the four-hour drive.

"Rarely. He likes to say that Mohammed comes to the mountain. The mountain doesn't come to Mohammed [sic]."

The Islamic reference did not make me feel any better about meeting him. I do not handle over-inflated egos well.

When we finally drove up to his house, and before I could even remove our luggage from the car, a huge hunk of man exploded out of the front door. Giving Tina hugs and kisses, he easily picked her up two feet off the ground. Then he stared me up and down, particularly my beard.

"I've heard a lot about you. Did you forget your razor?"

I let that one pass with a polite "no," just as he extended his hand and gave me a bone-crushing handshake that did not seem to end.

"And I've heard a lot about you as well," I said, trying not to wince.

His high apple cheeks shined, and his grin extended across his square jaw and face. I glanced at his gray hair, firmly in place with some sort of sweet smelling cream or gel.

"And here's, my wife, Jeannie," he waved as she sauntered out of the door, vodka and tonic in hand. She was a tall, thin, weathered woman; her glazed eyes told me this was not her first drink of the day.

"Come in ya'll," she said.

No sooner were we in the front door and I had dropped our luggage, did she say, "Now what can I get you to drink?"

Tina opted for a diet coke and I for an iced tea. It was 11:30 a.m.

"Oh come on now. I have mimosas already mixed up in the kitchen," she said.

Tina glanced at me, and we said, "Okay then."

As we moved to the backyard and sat under a pergola near the pool, I could tell that Bruce was meticulous. The pool was crystal clear with not even one leaf floating around. The landscaping was well trimmed and colorful. I inhaled the honeysuckle smells as I gazed out at the purple and red bougainvilleas and pink pentas plants. Also called "Egyptian Starflowers," their sweet nectar attracted bees, butterflies, and even hummingbirds. As Jeannie brought us our drinks, I watched a black and yellow monarch butterfly hover near one of the plants.

We sat under the wooden slatted roof, covered with laurel and ivy, below a large stag horn fern nailed to the wall, as a Hunter fan twirled above us, stirring up the heavy air.

"I hope you didn't eat yet," Bruce started. "Jeannie made her famous French toast with sausage and hash browns."

Tina answered for us. "No, we're starving. Do you need any help?"

"No. Ya'll just sit there. I'll let Moose entertain you," she quipped before disappearing into the kitchen.

Bruce Ackerson was a large man. He was large not only in stature, standing about six feet, five inches, but in presence as well. His presence commanded attention from everyone in a room as his booming voice and big arms draped over every one of the numerous family and friends who might be there. Having played football at West Point, he left the army as a Lieutenant Colonel. He wanted to stay in the service, but Helen convinced him to leave. He later became a stockbroker for Merrill-Lynch. Due to his size, family and friends simply called him "Moose."

In 1965 Bruce and Helen Ackerson, along with their eleven children, moved from New Jersey to St. Petersburg, Florida. They purchased a huge old Spanish-style home on Villa Grande Avenue

South, near Boca Ciega Bay and the stylish "Jungle" area in the western part of the city. Paved with old red brick stones, and ensconced by bougainvillea plants and huge old southern oak and pine trees, many of the waterfront homes there had been kept by the same families for generations.

Two years later, Bruce and Helen divorced, and both re-married within one year. Bruce moved out and his ex-wife, Helen re-married Victor Morgan, who moved in. However, unable to afford the sprawling property, Helen and Victor moved to Lakeland, where they rented a home on Live Oak Road and he took a job as a journalist with the Lakeland Ledger.

Bruce was a man of curious extremes. Born of Swedish ancestry, he was raised with a military mentality. He could be harsh with his children, like the time he caught his oldest son, Bud, smoking cigarettes as a teenager and startled sisters watched as he was flung over a car. Or when his daughter, Sue slipped out the f-word and got a hand across her face in a nanosecond. And yet under the rough exterior, there was a kindness and unending love of family that would often bring him to tears. When Sue was working in South Florida part-time at the Turkey Point nuclear power plant, he would get up with her at four a.m. to make coffee, breakfast, and pack her a lunch. Sue also reflected how he would meet her dates at the front door swinging a baseball bat as a warning of what might befall them if they tried any hanky-panky with his daughter.

He could be generous or miserly. He was openly racist, homophobic, and an incorrigible flirt with just about anything wearing a skirt. He was furious with some gay neighbors who flew a rainbow flag on their house instead of the American flag. Yet when he had a massive heart attack and a cardiac arrest, it was those same gay neighbors who immediately called 911 and saved his life.

He always needed to be the center of the crowd and would need little reason at family gatherings to stand up and make a speech. I remember being horrified at my wedding to his daughter when he stood up to make a toast at the reception and ended the long-winded oratory with this pomposity, "And finally I would like to thank my daughter for marrying a rich doctor!"

There was something unnerving about being with him. Perhaps it was his size or thunderous voice. Or maybe it was the plethora of prejudices and judgments. Or maybe it was his constant companion, Jeannie, who annoyed me. I couldn't put my finger on it until the mountain finally came to Mohammed.

Shortly after our daughter, Emily, was born, they drove up for a visit. They planned to stay for one night and then drive further north to visit Tina's sister, Sue, in Dunnellon. As Bruce swaddled my baby daughter is his large arms, I saw a side of him that his children recognized—kind and gentle. Emily looked up at him and cooed, as he sang an off-key nursery rhyme. As Tina and I prepared dinner, Jeannie got drunk quicker than a furloughed sailor.

We never kept much liquor in the house, only beer and wine. However, in preparation for the visit, Tina had purchased a half-gallon of vodka. Jeannie was devouring it like water. The more she drank, the more obnoxious she became.

"So how many more children are you going to have?" Jeannie asked me.

"I already have two other daughters, so I am not sure…"

She didn't even let me finish before spitting out, "Oh come on now. Look at how beautiful Emily is…you can't stop with just one."

Tina blushed and said nothing. It got worse.

"You're a doctor! I'm sure you can afford it."

Bruce finally interceded. "I think it might be time for bed. We've had a long day."

Clearly Jeannie wasn't finished yet.

"I just meant they should have a big family."

He rose and firmly grabbed her arm and led her to the guest bedroom, where she promptly passed out.

Tina and I looked at each other and the almost depleted vodka bottle.

Later in bed as she nursed Emily, Tina said, "I apologize for Jeannie's behavior. That's how she is. None of us can stand her really."

The next morning Bruce took Tina aside and apologized for his wife's performance last evening, thanked me for our hospitality, and said they needed to get on the road soon. Jeannie stumbled out of the guest bathroom, her black and gray short hair freshly washed, and bags under her eyes the size of potato sacks. She gulped coffee in an effort to tame her hangover, and was quiet and subdued.

I saw Bruce for what he was—an old-fashioned bigoted military man, but with a kind soul, who loved his family. It was just his choice in wives that seemed flawed. With what I was about to experience in the future, my choices seemed no better. Perhaps it was this revelation that was touching a nerve inside of me, and my discomfort was starting to surface.

The memories of this iconic man were remarkably similar from all of his children. His oldest daughter Pam recalled how he took her to a Notre Dame Father/Daughter Dance and afterword out for dinner. "You would have thought I was his only child."

"He was always my hero and sat at the right hand of God," Pam continued, "but the memory that forever sealed his fate as my idol was when I became pregnant at age seventeen. I was 'sent away' to New Smyrna. I had never been away from my family, so I was afraid and wanting my mother, who would not speak to me. My dad was the only family I saw the entire time. He would bring presents...silly things that made me laugh. I was so ashamed and didn't want him to see me, but he came at least three times a month and made me feel good and clean and worthy. He always said, 'to forgive is to forget,' meaning never to throw it back in one's face."

Like Sue, Pam compared him to the television legendary ultra-conservative icon, Archie Bunker. One time, her brother, Chip, showed up for a visit with Moose, who wouldn't let him into the house because he looked like a "long-haired hippie faggot." Unlike a fine wine, he did not "mellow" with age. Yet, Bruce Ackerson was a man of conviction, gregarious, loyal, honest and fun loving.

"He had a huge capacity for love, making us feel cherished," Pam recalled.

Janey's memories of her father were wonderful, and she recalls sitting on his lap when she was five years old as he read the newspaper to her. She, like all the other children, had a standing offer to move to Hollywood, Florida to live with him at anytime. She was torn with the decision, but ultimately decided to stay in St. Petersburg, because she said, "I couldn't leave my grandmother and mother." She had seen first hand what Vic could do to both of them. Probably as important was the fact that she was dating Dick, her future husband, whom she married when she was only seventeen, just to get out of the abusive home. Although her protective instincts may have influenced her decision to stay, ironically she lost contact with her family when she started having children.

"I felt guilty for having healthy children. Chip had lost a baby, and Sue had just had her second son, who was born with a disability (spina bifida). Finally, I got over this and brought my kids down often to Hollywood where he would love them very much. I started another wonderful relationship with my dad then. Towards the end of his life we were going down about every two weeks, and then every week, just before he died. He adored Kelly, (one of her daughters), and she would spend all of her time with him. She would brush his hair, rub his feet, and feed him. They were very close, and I am grateful she had time with him."

She also recalled him visiting her workplace in St. Petersburg, and how "the women would go crazy. He would flirt with them and made them feel so special. He was a beautiful man."

In a cruel twist of fate, or bad karma, the children who he so loved and tried to protect, would ultimately suffer abuse at the hands of their new alcoholic stepfather, who was also a pedophile. Through multiple interviews with the surviving children, I do not believe that Bruce was ever made fully aware of the abuse at the time it was occurring. It was not something his daughters ever spoke about until much later in life. The children would often call Bruce in his new home in Hollywood, Florida about the new stepdad being mean and prone to violence. Yet the few times he would drive the four hours back to St. Petersburg, Helen and Vic would get wind of it, and everything seemed normal by the time he arrived. The sisters were warned of physical punishment if they ever told their dad what was really happening. And yet, as a father myself, I find it difficult to believe that he was totally ignorant of the appalling conditions in which his children were being raised.

Eventually, four of the younger children went to live with their father in South Florida, but found his military discipline, and their new stepmother's excessive drinking, only slightly more hospitable. Sadly, Bruce would not find out about the sexual abuse for decades, after Tina died. By then, the secret pain harbored by the children could no longer be contained, and their delayed rage and need for redemption were unleashed.

Happy Days

————————

At around seven p.m. on October 17, 1989, Tina, my best friend Steve Greenberg, and I were pummeling crab claws with a wooden hammer and throwing back some beers at Crabby Bill's, a well known Indian Rocks Beach bar and restaurant. The television over the bar blasted taped play from the World Series in San Francisco. The Oakland Athletics were due to play the San Francisco Giants in that night's opening game of the series. We had just finished eating dinner and were shooting hoops at the miniature basketball court inside the restaurant. Just after eight o'clock, the television feed began to shake and break up. We looked up at the screen and heard sportscaster Al Michaels say, "I'll tell you what—we're having an earth—." At that moment, the feed from Candlestick Park was lost. The network put up a green ABC Sports graphic as the audio was switched to a telephone link. Michaels cracked, "Well, folks, that's the greatest open in the history of television, bar none!" His voice was accompanied by the cheering of fans who had no idea of the devastation elsewhere in the city.

Steve looked at us. "Isn't that where you're going for your honeymoon next week?"

I looked at Tina and we both nodded our heads.

As we watched the news over the ensuing days, we talked it over and decided to stick with the plan. Having both lived in California at separate times in our lives, we were no strangers to earthquakes and knew there would be aftershocks. However, I felt that the risk of another major quake so soon was low.

————————

Our wedding was held at the beautiful Bellair Country Club in Clearwater, Florida, an old historic wooden building sitting on high ground overlooking the Gulf of Mexico. Our plans had been for an outdoor wedding, however a brief afternoon shower forced us inside. Both of our immediate and extended families were there. A very reformed Rabbi did the short service and after stomping on the glass with my heel in accordance with an ancient Jewish tradition, the celebration began.

Champagne and wine were plentiful everywhere as the band played the 1979 song, "We Are Family." And what a family it was—fourteen from my side and forty-two Ackerson family, spouses, and children. As the music and drinks heated up, everyone was dancing—including my medical partners. Dr. John Finn, who had just joined my medical group even danced and said this was the first time he and his wife Gloria had danced since their wedding.

One of the high points was a Conga line that threaded throughout the whole ballroom as we swerved and kicked to "Feeling Hot, Hot, Hot." After what seemed like the hundredth verse of "Ole, Ole," my brother and Steve signaled everyone to form a circle for the traditional Jewish wedding and celebration song, the Horah. The guests circle the wedding couple, hold hands and side step and kick in alternating directions while singing in Hebrew lyrics that most people don't understand. To start the dance, everybody forms a circle, holding hands, and steps forward toward the right with the left foot, and then follows with the right foot. The left foot is then brought back, followed by the right foot. This is done while holding hands and circling together in a fast and cheerful motion to the right. Large groups allow for the creation of several concentric circles.

"More circles," my sister Susan yelled clapping her hands high in the air.

Tina and I were pushed to the center of the circle and placed on chairs as several hefty male guests hoisted us in the air. The Ackerson clan enjoyed the Jewish tradition so much that they proceeded to hoist other members of my family above the dancing crowd. The wedding photographer snapped one picture of my youngest daughter Sarah being raised above the fray by Tina's brother Bud and her father, Bruce, (see back book cover).

"Havah Negelia!" Sarah screamed.

"More dancing!" Tina yelled as the exhausted crowd collapsed after never ending verses of the Israeli celebration song. As the band busted out with "Love Shack" by the B-52's, people caught a second wind. Ties and jackets were ripped off and left on chairs, and more champagne was poured. Another crowd, including Tina and her sisters, began to twirl in the center. Off balance, one of Tina's brothers stepped on her right foot, and she wobbled like a duck with a wounded wing.

I was at the main table taking a water break and chatting with my family when Tina's sister Jodi came over and told me there might be a problem. I looked up and saw her limping to the sidelines.

"Let me take a look," I said to her just as she dropped into a chair.

"It's probably nothing," she said.

I removed her shoe and gently pressed the top of her foot that caused some wincing.

"It could just be a bruise," I said, "or a small fracture. I think more dancing is out."

Sweaty and drunk, she threw her head back and laughed.

"Keep an eye on her," I said to Jodi. "Whatever she says—no more dancing."

She never got an X-Ray, but I suspected a small fracture later since on our honeymoon, the top of her foot turned black and blue and she limped up the hills of San Francisco.

Next came all of the toasts and my new father-in-law's infamous and embarrassing line about how lucky *he* was that his daughter was marrying a "rich doctor." By that point, I had consumed enough alcohol to just drop my eyes and head downward and shake it back and forth. I was stunned and speechless.

Stumbling into our honeymoon suite after midnight, we trampled over soft rose petals covering the floor and the bed, and I ravenously tore off her cream colored wedding gown. I was sober enough however to notice that her skin oozed vapors of alcohol, but I didn't care. We made love and promptly passed out. Hung over and groggy, we had brunch the next day with our out of town families and then took a limousine to the airport. The black stretch limo was lined with white crepe paper and the requisite "Just Married" sign on the back window. The limo company had supplied a bottle of champagne, which we both declined. We slept most of the way on the plane to San Francisco.

We had chosen our honeymoon in the bay area based upon reports and personal knowledge of October being one of the more pleasant weather times in Northern California. After checking into our B&B, we headed for Chinatown.

Outside the Lichee Garden Restaurant on Powell Street, we were both overtaken by the sweet and pungent smell of Dim Sum, the authentic Chinese cooking style where various dishes are prepared in large quantity and then pushed around on metal carts with steam baskets on top. You get to look and smell and pick the ones you want. At the end of the meal, the waiter simply adds up your plates and presents a bill.

While we sipped a spicy white California wine, Caymus Conundrum, we enjoyed barbeque pork in soft steamed dough shells, mini spare ribs, and fried shrimp with a Sichuan sauce.

"I don't think I can eat anymore," I said, as I pushed back from the table, still sipping my wine.

"This is the best food I've ever had. Thank you so much," Tina replied. "I don't think I can ever go home." Her blue-green eyes were twinkling.

"You'll just have to learn to cook Dim Sum I guess," I said.

As we left and walked over to Grant Street, we shopped for teapots and smelled all kinds of loose-leaf black teas with scents of jasmine, citrus and malts and the green teas released aromas of ginseng and flowers. Loaded with bags of teas and accessories, we exited into the crisp, warm fall air.

"I think we should give the white teapot to your mother," I said.

But as I turned to Tina, I noticed that she had fallen back to stop by a doorway where an oriental beggar woman in rags squatted with a tin cup in one hand and a sleeping infant ensconced in a dark gray woolen blanket resting in the other. She placed both the infant and the cup down and then clasped her hands together, nodding her head to thank the kind stranger, albeit in Mandarin.

"What are you doing?" I asked.

"I'm giving her some money."

"Why?"

"Why not? Can't you tell that she needs it? Just look at her," she pleaded.

"I can't tell if she needs money. Maybe she's a con artist who would rather beg than work for a living. How much did you give her?"

"Oh, David, just look at her, will you?" she implored with an outstretched hand, tears welling up in her eyes.

As I watched her reach into her purse and pull out a twenty-dollar bill, I grabbed Tina's hand.

"We're going," I said.

As Tina complied, the disheveled woman grabbed her other arm, while still supporting the sleeping baby, and a tug-of-war ensued. She kissed the back of Tina's hand gently, still nodding, praying, and now crying, I was able to finally extract her from the beggar's grip. As we walked away, tears streamed form Tina's eyes.

"Have you always been that generous?" I asked.

"Yes," she said. "Always."

I did not argue as I could see that she was genuinely touched and charitable.

"Even when you were poor?"

"Even more when I was poor, because I know what hunger and pain is and I don't want anyone to suffer if I can help."

"But you can't feed the world," I argued.

"Oh honey, I'm not trying to feed the world, just the world that touches me." And to this, I had no answer.

I let go of her arm and signaled her with my eyes. She immediately walked back to the woman and gave her the money.

As it would turn out, most tourists had been scared off by the news reports and endless loop of the same waterfront fire. To watch the evening news, one would have thought that the entire city was burning. Nothing could have been further from the truth. We walked all around the city and saw little structural damage. Other than the locals, it was like a ghost town. We got into the top restaurants without a reservation, and often had an entire dining room to ourselves.

The next day, we drove over the Golden Gate Bridge, and visited Muir Woods, the giant redwood trees, and our ultimate destination— Sonoma County and the wine country. Everyday was a visit to two or three wineries and picnics outside with fresh baked breads, cheeses, meats, fruits, multicolored Heirloom tomatoes, and limited release bottles of all kinds of red wine and white varietals and blends. Dinners were gastronomic events with eye and taste bud appealing dishes, from pumpkin soup with goat cheese cream and thyme croutons to local Petaluma chicken breasts stuffed with artichokes, apples, and cranberries. Desserts were to die for: warm Valrhona chocolate cake with homemade vanilla bean ice cream, or twice-baked apple cobbler with Pinot Noir Ice Wine reduction sauce. I had never felt happier—being with this woman, in one of the most idyllic locations in the country, and enjoying the finest food and wine I had ever experienced. This was bliss.

Once back home, we settled into a newlywed routine as Tina

moved into my three-bedroom condo in Bardmoor. We decorated and opened wedding presents as she wrote thank-you notes. We both worked full-time and had my girls for dinner every Wednesday night and every other weekend. Their bond with Tina strengthened as they slowly came to accept that she wasn't the enemy. Barbara, to her credit, did not paint Tina as the proverbial "home-wrecker,"—at least not in front of our children. Dinners were usually homemade and of epic quality. We subscribed to Bon Apetit and Gourmet magazines, and would make countless new meals, always with a bottle of wine. There were memorable meals like grouper with orange-Grand Marnier sauce and vegetables in parchment paper, or homemade spring rolls and jerk chicken. We were so good in the kitchen that friends were afraid of inviting us over for dinner, fearing the inevitable comparison.

One night after dinner, we were both standing near the sink, cleaning up dishes. Tina seemed sullen and quiet. I had the sense she might want to talk.

"A penny for your thoughts?" I asked.

Taking a long sip of her ever present, and never empty, wine glass, she hesitated a bit, and then started to speak.

"My Mom just called and said Vic, (her stepfather), needs open heart surgery."

Until this point, she had spoken little about him and I felt there might be more.

"How do you feel about that?" I asked.

"I'm not sure," she answered. "My mom loves him but he did a lot of bad things to us when we were growing up."

I was now certain a raw nerve was being touched. I moved on with caution. Taking a wet pot from her hand, I dried and laid it on the counter. I reached for her hand and led her out to the couch in the family room.

"Do you want to talk about it?" I asked.

She drew in some air in what appeared to be a half sigh and half deep breath. Her lower lip quivered.

"Vic and mom used to drink—a lot. He's been sober now for over thirty years. He was a mean drunk. He would beat us, my mom, and even my grandmother. God help you if you crossed him while he was drinking."

I knew there was more—much more. What came out next caught

me completely off guard.

"When I was only eight, Vic forced me to drink vodka. If I refused, he would beat me with his belt. Then when I was twelve, he raped me."

I sat dumbfounded in silence. To my surprise she wasn't crying. The story just spilled out with all of the detached emotion of a television newscaster.

"Did you tell anyone?" I asked.

"Only my sister Pam, but she didn't believe me. He told me that if I told anyone he would know, and then he would beat up my mom even more. All of us were afraid of him."

"Then what happened?" I asked

"I think Pam must have said something to Bud and Chip (her two oldest brothers). They confronted Vic the next day and a fight broke out. He never touched me again."

"That's terrible," I said in earnest. "So you never told your mom?"

"No, what good would it have done?" she shrugged.

I couldn't believe what I was hearing and said, "Maybe he would have been arrested and no one else would have been hurt. Did he abuse anyone else?"

She raised her shoulders as if to fend off any further discussion. Her only reply was, "Oh well, what's done is done I guess."

One night, about a year into our marriage, Tina said to me, "Can we make a baby?"

Having discussed this before we wed, I had expected the question. My practice was thriving and I had finally paid off all of my legal bills. I wasn't getting any younger, and I would do anything to make her happy.

"Okay," I said. "When do you want to start?"

She rose from her chair and moved toward me seductively, shedding her blouse and bra. As she dangled an ample breast in my face, she answered, "How about now?"

It didn't take long for the home pregnancy test to turn positive. We called all of our family and started to plan a new home. In 1990 the link between alcohol and fetal abnormalities was just becoming known, and for the first time, I started to worry and monitor her drinking. She reduced her wine consumption, but never really quit drinking all together. When I would bring up the subject, she would immediately dismiss it with the wave of her hand.

"The doctors say you're not supposed to drink while you're pregnant," I would say.

"Doctors—poppycock! What do they know? My mother and grandmother both drank wine while they were pregnant, and we all turned out just fine."

I had no answer to that and therefore rationalized that she was indeed drinking at a greatly reduced level, so I just let it go. Deep down, however, I worried about the health of my yet unborn child, despite reassuring ultrasounds, (the first of which confirmed the normal development of my soon to be third daughter), and an amniocentesis. During the last procedure, where a small ultrasound-guided needle is inserted into the pregnant woman's belly, and amniotic fluid is withdrawn for analysis, I watched in fascination as the tip of the sharp object almost touched my daughter's hand. Then I promptly fainted. With smelling salts under my nose, I awakened to the obstetrician chuckling, "So, does this happen to you often at work?"

Embarrassed, I could only say, "No."

Tina worked full-time until her last month of pregnancy. Emily had striking red hair right out of the chute. My older girls, Rachel and Sarah, took an immediate liking to her, and helped out whenever they were over for a visit. Tina was an instant breast-feeding machine, enjoying the whole "stay at home mom thing." She quit work, and continued to enjoy her evening wine, stating it would relax her and the baby as well. The pediatrician advised against any alcohol while breast-feeding; however, since Emily's development was perfectly normal, I again couldn't argue.

All of Tina's sisters would visit—Pam, Sue, Janey, Mary, Meighan and Jodi. They all fawned over and spoiled the new baby. Meighan's two girls, Brittany and Kristin, would hold her like a doll and play with her like their own sister.

Emily started preschool and Tina's drinking gradually increased, but went largely unnoticed by me. At first, she was an excellent mother, showering our daughter with the most expensive clothes from Neiman Marcus and Oilily. She had professional photographs made of the two of them, in warm and classical sepia tones, and the interior of our home was plastered with portraits and photographs of our daughter. Tina continued to cook gourmet meals like snapper with guava-lime glaze, and orzo with wild mushrooms. There was of course, always one beautiful bottle of wine with dinner.

Yet, something strange was happening right under my nose, and I didn't notice it until the problem became too big to ignore. As a friend would later tell me, "it's easier to see the trees if you are standing outside, not inside, the forest." By the time it became too obvious to ignore it was too late.

Darkness

———～◦✦◦～———

For the first two years of Emily's life, the three of us seemed like the ideal family. Tina showered her with the finest of everything—determined for her not to have the kind of impoverished childhood she had suffered. More than once I had heard Tina's tales of not having enough food to eat and dry milk being diluted with lots of water to feed eleven hungry mouths. I therefore simply took for granted her overcompensation when it came to Emily's clothes and meals proportioned more for six people than three. We built our dream house in Seminole, Florida on a cul-de-sac of only a dozen homes, on a heavily wooded lot of old Southern Oaks, dripping with Spanish moss and slash pines. We had a screened-in pool and an ample yard where I constructed an herb garden raised on old railroad ties with a drip irrigation system. We completed our "Rockwellian" family unit with a rescued mix-breed terrier, named "Lucky." Everything seemed perfectly normal to me at first. However, growing insidiously inside Tina was a diabolic enemy. The clues started to become too obvious to ignore—even to me.

Upon coming home, I found Emily unkempt and dinners not prepared as promised. I would call Tina in the afternoon and discover her napping, or not making much sense when she spoke. The garage door and side door of the house were left open in the heat of summer, and laundry went undone—something she had formerly been meticulous in addressing. The thought that she was drunk had not even crossed my mind—until one pivotal night.

After a dinner, which we both prepared, Emily was in the family room watching a Disney videotape of "Beauty and the Beast." As Tina was finishing the dishes, she was unusually quiet, normally preferring to chatter, even if I wasn't paying attention. I was at the kitchen bar reading a fishing magazine. The cool granite counter reflected water dripping from my iced-beer mug, highlighted by the overhead hanging spotlights.

"I think I'm an alcoholic," she said.

Dumbfounded, blindsided, and speechless, I don't recall what I said in response. My mind raced and tried to compute her statement, but it kept coming up blank. Analytical and linear of thought, I could always frame and formulate any problem, and possible solutions, instantly. But for this, I had neither foundation nor experience upon which to draw. At that moment, my world stopped. In retrospect, the impact upon me could only be compared to my ex-wife's confession of infidelity.

I muttered something lame like, "So what are you going to do about that?"

She shrugged her shoulders, eyes staring down at a pot dripping water in a drain board next to the stainless steel sink.

As a physician, I had treated many alcoholics, but the mere thought that I was married to one was not even on my radar screen. No. Not possible, I thought. This must be a mistake or even a bad joke. But suddenly the reality started to crystallize. The naps, the absent household chores, and missed appointments fit perfectly.

"Why don't you just stop drinking?" I asked.

I was in major denial and unwilling to accept this possibility until slammed over the head with it. As fate would have it, that wouldn't take long.

"I don't know," she answered in a muted voice. I sat at the bar, surprised and speechless. She silently continued to wash the dishes.

"Kill the beast!" blared ironically in the background, as Emily sat transfixed, eyes intent on the screen, and oblivious to her parents' conversation.

Insomnia had never been a problem for me, but that night I could not sleep. Finally getting up, I read a medical journal and watched the rodeo on ESPN, but could not shake the growing agitation inside, replaying the short conversation over and over in my head. It was impossible, I thought. Sure she liked to drink, but this was my wife, my dream, my world, whom I adored and loved. Hell, I never even had a friend or family member who was an alcoholic. Those were dropouts from society—bums and homeless people who panhandled on the street corner. They were confined to insane asylums or medical wards where they threw up blood, had DT's, and seized until they died. No, this could not be my wife.

Over the ensuing weeks, I did and said nothing to her about her drinking problem. My work became a distraction from my problems at home, and those were escalating at a rapid pace. There were few meals prepared, little laundry done, and Emily's toilet training had gone in reverse. As I did more and more of the cooking, Tina's sleeping increased and her food intake was almost nonexistent. My specialty and her favorite—rice risotto, even went untouched.

The deterioration in her health had been so insidious that it went largely unnoticed by me—ironic—a doctor. Much like a frog placed into a pot of cold water, with the heat slowly turning up, I didn't realize things were terribly wrong, until well, they were terribly wrong. Tina was gaining weight, but hid it well. Her belly and legs began to swell, which were telltale signs of liver failure. Her eyes yellowed, and even as a doctor, my mind consistently rejected the truth.

"I think you need to see a doctor," I finally said one day.

"I'm married to one," she retorted.

"Right," I responded. "I mean a gastroenterologist." We had had this conversation several times in recent weeks and yet she remained resistant. Worn down, one day, she finally relented.

"Okay, fine. I'll do it. Who?"

"How about Heidi Goldberg? She's young, bright, and honest." And also a no-nonsense "tells it like it is bitch," I thought. She would set Tina straight, not mince words, and really kick her ass sober. Or at least so I imagined. Scribbling her phone number on a piece of scrap paper, I slid it over the kitchen counter towards her.

"Fine. I'll call her," she said. She stood in defiance with arms folded across her chest.

⸻

"What's this for?" I asked the following week, picking up a bottle of Xanax from the bathroom counter.

"So I can stop drinking without withdrawal," Tina replied.

"You're kidding, right? You're going to try detoxing at home?"

"Sure. Why not? You think I can't do it?"

Saying nothing, I just shook my head in complete befuddlement, and walked away. Picking up the portable phone, I went outside by the pool, and dialed Heidi's number.

"Heidi, this is David. You saw Tina yesterday, correct?"

"Yes," she said.

"Did you give her Xanax and tell her to stop drinking at home?" I asked.

Blunt and direct, she cut to the chase. "Look, I tried to get her to go into the hospital. She's very sick. She has advanced alcoholic cirrhosis possibly mixed with hepatitis, and needs immediate in-patient care. She may even need a liver transplant. However, she refused to be admitted. She's in denial. What else could I do?"

Collecting my thoughts for a moment, I replied, "Nothing. I guess. I'll speak with her. By the way, thanks for seeing her on such short notice."

When confronted with Heidi's recommendation, Tina's answer was short—"No."

Several nights later after a Christmas party at her sister Meighan's house, Tina stumbled out to the car, ataxic and mumbling, as I held Emily in my arms.

"How much did you have to drink tonight?"

"Nothing," she said with slurred speech.

"Then why are you bumping and weaving all over the parking lot?"

"Oh please stop nagging me, it's just the Xanax I took." Dubious, I almost bought the lie. Not until one week later did events spiral so out of control that my world imploded. I could no longer deny that life, at least as I had known it, had ended, and would never be the same.

———————

When we first met, Tina's only sister who lived in St. Pete was Janey. Tina was very close to her and her four children; however, for me she remained guarded and a mystery. When we would get together at family gatherings and holidays, her husband, Dickie, was almost never with her. She would say he did not like to attend family events. When he would appear, he stood out from the other men—crass, crude and overweight. He would have a beer in one hand and a cigarette in another. He had a vile view of women.

"Hey Brittany, you're looking fine these days," he would leer at one of his nieces with a twisted sneer.

Brittany Perry, who was only twelve at the time of the comment, shot back, "Thanks, Uncle Dick." She would then move away from him as fast and as far as possible.

In truth, I think Janey encouraged him not to show up at family functions to save herself the embarrassment. Any information I had about her and her marriage, Tina parceled out to me in small doses.

"Janey's not really happy, although she appears to be," Tina would often say.

"Then why does she stay with him?" I'd ask.

Tina would hold her first three fingers in the air and rub them together.

"Money. She's afraid if she leaves him she'll have no money for herself or her kids."

Her relationship with Janey was complex. At times she had nothing but loving comments about her sister, and at other times expressed nothing but disdain.

"She's my favorite sister," she would say one night, and then another time she would opine, "At least I didn't run off when I was seventeen to marry the bug man." (Dickie was in the pest control business.) Later it would become much clearer to me why she had run away and married this guy.

By 1990 one of her younger sisters, Meighan, moved from Hollywood, Florida to St. Pete, taking a job as a neo-natal intensive care unit nurse at All Children's Hospital. Petite and playful, Meighan was the family jokester. Her way of dealing with her traumatic past was humor—dark humor. Her first husband Phil Perry was a cop with the Hollywood Police Department, and they had two beautiful daughters, Brittany and Kristin.

Before moving to St. Pete, she would make the two hundred and fifty mile trip in a little bit over three hours. When I asked her how she did it, she would say, "We don't even stop to pee."

"What about your girls?" I asked referring to Brittany and Kristin who were two and three years old at the time.

A devilish grin appeared and she said, "Oh I just knock them out with baby Ativan (a sedative)." I believe she was telling the truth.

———————

One day, Tina had not answered the phone all afternoon, so I decided to go home early from work. The smoke detector was screeching as I walked into the house. Opening all the doors and windows immediately, I saw smoke arising from the kitchen range, where an empty burning pot had been left on the stove. Tina was passed out on the couch. I removed the ember-encased pot with a large asbestos potholder, and silenced the wailing alarm.

"Where is Emily?" I yelled at her—no response. I walked over and shook her.

She snapped awake and said, "Next door at Samantha's house playing. Why?"

Samantha Staub lived three houses down from us on a small cul-de-sac, named Drew Oaks Drive. Emily would often be over there playing.

"I was just wondering, since the smoke alarm was going off. Are you trying to burn down the house?" I asked, enraged.

"No. I'm sorry. I must have fallen asleep."

I could feel my face getting hot and my blood pressure rising. "You're drunk, aren't you?"

"NO! I just took some pills to help me stop drinking."

"What pills?"

She shoved a bottle of tranquilizers towards me, but as I drew near, the stench of alcohol was unmistakable. I knew we were headed for a confrontation, but before I could say anything else, the phone rang.

"Hello," I snapped.

"David?" I recognized Meighan's voice. "She's been drinking a lot, hasn't she?"

"I guess so. I don't see any evidence of it though."

"Search the house," she pleaded. "She's got to be hiding it somewhere. I have been trying to reach her all day and I'm really worried."

"Me too. I came home and the house was almost burned down," I exaggerated.

Tina had passed out again, so I embarked on a room-by-room search without her. I went through every bathroom, kitchen cabinet, and even opened the tank on the back of the master bathroom toilet. Frustrated, I finally entered her walk-in closet. There were new and dirty clothes strewn everywhere on the floor. I peaked at shelves, flipping through rows of new designer clothes and jeans with the tags still attached—nothing.

With my hands on my hips and sweating, my eyes were somehow drawn to a tall brown wicker laundry basket, where underneath a pile of clothes, I found the mother lode. There were empty cans of beer and two empty gallon jugs of cheap white wine. I went ballistic. Grabbing one of the empty bottles, I stormed into the family room, thinking I might smash the bottle across her face. Fortunately, by the time I reached her, I was able to calm down a notch.

"So, you're not drunk, huh? Then what the fuck do you call this?" I yelled, waving the bottle close to her nose. There was no answer. Her eyes were glazed and a stream of rheum fell from the corner of her mouth. The house was silent and I heard a crow cawing outside.

"This game is over. You're going to the hospital now, then straight to rehab."

"No," she stammered.

"You're going whether you want to or not."

Propped up precariously on one elbow, she started to cry. As she blew her nose, blood started to ooze out, and I saw an opportunity. I handed her a handkerchief.

"Thank you," she said.

"Well?" I asked, waiting in silence. "This is your last chance to go voluntarily."

She stared at me in silent defiance, eyes bloodshot and half-closed.

I reached for the phone and dialed 911.

Hearing me talk to the 911 operators, Tina awakened and bolted towards the door. I hung up immediately and grabbed her purse so she couldn't drive. She pushed by me and went out the door, just missing a wall. I went back to pick up the phone as the operator kept saying, "Hello, hello..." Before the ambulance could arrive, she disappeared into the night. A trail of blood led out of the front door, and with ambulance sirens screaming, I suddenly felt duped. As the paramedics got out of the ambulance, and approached me, I told them she was drunk, had liver failure, and was bleeding profusely. (I exaggerated in the hope that they would be forced to take her to the hospital—that is once we found her.) When it came to the part about where she was, I had to admit, "I don't know." Looking at each other, they told me that even if she turned up, they could not force her to go to the hospital. Nodding, I thanked them for coming. After they left, I looked around the outside of the house.

"If you don't come out, I'm going to call the police," I said to the bushes, and then felt like even more of a raving lunatic. Hearing rustling, I parted some oleanders, only to see a feral cat dart out. Walking around the back of the house likewise produced nothing, so I went back to the front of the house and found her sitting on the ground in the middle of the cul-de-sac. As I approached her, she said, "I'm not going."

Grabbing her arm, I tried to pull her up. She reached over to me with her other hand and clawed at my neck with her nails, screeching, "No!"

I let go and stomped back inside and called the police. If the ambulance wouldn't take her, maybe the cops would. Speaking to the police operator, I hatched a plan.

"Pinellas County Sheriff, may I help you?" the dull and stiff voice on the other end of the phone said.

"Yes. My name is David Mokotoff and I would like to file a domestic violence report."

"Who is the victim?"

Realizing that she would probably not believe me, I paused momentarily and then said, "Me. My wife's an alcoholic, is drunk and bleeding and just attacked me. The paramedics said they could only take her to the hospital if she consented."

"And did she refuse?"

"Yes. Hence the altercation."

"Did you strike her?"

"No."

Skeptical, but reluctant not to act, she finally took all the information and promised that a squad car would be out shortly.

Tina was still squatting in the middle of the street as a police car pulled up. After hearing the story, the two cops kneeled to talk to her. She looked up at me, and for the first time, I did not recognize her. I had never seen her look so pitiful, disheveled, and defeated. Her bleeding had subsided. Supporting both of her arms, the officers helped her up, escorted her to the back of the squad car, lowered her head as she went inside, and then drove off. After calling Samantha's mom, Eileen, and explaining the emergency, they agreed to watch Emily for the night. I then drove to the hospital emergency room.

In the ER, she alternately flirted and verbally abused the admitting nurse and doctor. I felt embarrassed and nauseated. Her bleeding was minimal; however, her blood counts and chemistries were quite deranged due to her liver disease. Her admitting BAL, (blood alcohol level), was 3.0, which was more than three times the legal limit for a DUI. I quickly placed a call to Heidi Goldberg's answering service, asking them to have her call me back "stat." A few minutes later she called me on my mobile phone.

"I have Tina here. She's been drinking and had a nosebleed. We got into a fight and I had the police escort her to the ER. Her counts are out of whack and her BAL is 3.0."

"I'll be right in. Tell them to admit her to my service."

About thirty minutes later, she arrived, spoke to me briefly and then went to exam Tina. She was in the room for only fifteen minutes. When she came out she invited me into the doctors' dictation room and wasted no words.

"She's very sick. She's in hepatic failure. She needs blood and a platelet transfusion. She may have more serious bleeding soon."

I acknowledged what she had said without accepting the extent of the news.

I was bewildered—I knew she was sick, but I wasn't prepared for this extra bombshell. I just nodded my head in shocked silence, trying to digest the indigestible.

"I will get her sedated and admitted. She may go into DTs. Once she's stabilized, we will transfer her to a rehab facility."

"Aren't you going to scope her?" I asked, meaning passing a tube down her throat to exam the food pipe and stomach for bleeding sites.

"No. If she has varices and they're not bleeding yet, I could make the situation worse."

Varices are enlarged veins along the food pipe or esophagus. In a normal and healthy person, they are thinner than a pencil. However, when the liver becomes sick and hardened, the blood can no longer pass through it at the usual low pressure and so it backs up. These tender vessels then swell from the pressure, into the size of garden hoses. They are not made to handle the force, and eventually burst. It's how many alcoholics die. I again nodded, feeling numb.

"Now go home and get some rest. And I strongly suggest you do not do any heart caths for at least one week."

This was not what I wanted to hear, but reluctantly agreed not to place my patients in jeopardy. I would have to cancel procedures for tomorrow. As I got into my car to drive home, there was a very gentle rain falling with some fog, and I listened to the hypnotic sound of the wiper blades. Inside my car, it was just a trickle, but then it became a flood—I finally started to cry.

Entering the house, I could still smell stale beer and wine. I reached for the empty jug and hurled it towards the fireplace, where it smashed into thousands of pieces. Dripping with sweat and rainwater, I wandered to our bedroom and stripped out of my soggy clothes. Inside the walk-in shower, the warm water momentarily soothed me. Leaning against the wet tile wall, I began to cry again and repeated out loud, "Why me, Lord?"

Rehab

The next day I made what seemed like an endless number of phone calls to concerned family members, friends, and medical partners. The days fused into one another and became a blur. I took an extended leave of absence for one month, and my mother volunteered to fly down from New York to help out. I drove Emily to see her mother in the hospital, but could not fully explain to her why she was so sick. Tina would just cry and hold her baby. Like Michael Keaton in the movie, I was "Mr. Mom," and did shopping and cleaning and carpools. My mother and friends told me I should start looking for a nanny or au pair. Tina's bleeding stopped shortly after admission as more family and friends gathered. On day three, I walked into her room to find her sweating, tremulous, and shaking.

"Make them go away!"

"Make who go away?"

"The bugs—up there! Can't you see them?" Tina could not point because her wrists were tied to the side rails of the bed with cloth restraints, but she was still trying to sit up, buckling at the tie downs. The room smelled of feces and urine.

Looking up at the ceiling, I saw nothing. I felt her forehead—it was hot, so I went to find her nurse.

"I think she's got DTs," I said.

"Why do you say that?" she responded, clueless. I shot back, "Because she's febrile, has a rapid pulse, and is seeing bugs on the ceiling! Other than that, she seems fine. Now please call her doctor, and by the way, she needs to be cleaned up."

She nodded and scowled.

After several minutes, Heidi Goldberg called back an order for sedatives and more restraints. I decided to meet with her psychiatrist, an overweight man in his sixties, with a large white beard, who looked like Santa Claus. He had round, slightly tinted John Lennon eyeglasses and a polka-dot bowtie. He was direct.

"Your wife is in denial. She needs to be transferred to a drug and alcohol in-patient facility as soon as she is medically stable."

I nodded my head in agreement, asked for a list of rehab centers I could visit, and left the hospital. It was Christmas Eve day and everyone seemed to be in a holiday mood, except me. Being raised Jewish, Christmas had always made me feel sad, lonely, and like an outsider. As I walked to my silver Lexus coupe in the brightly–lit doctors' parking lot, I reflected even more about the holiday. Long ago I had grown used to a snowless winter. My first wife had been Jewish and we, and other members of our tribe, would have Christmas Eve dinner at a local Chinese restaurant. Over the years, I had granted Tina a tree with presents, and had spent several holidays with her family, but now I felt even more depressed and isolated. Playing the past few months over and over in my mind didn't help my sour mood much either. Distracted, I slammed into another parked car as I was leaving the lot. Although the damage was minor, I left a business card under the wiper blade, with a brief apology, and drove away.

Two days later, Tina had recovered from her DTs, stopped bleeding and recalled nothing. She finally agreed to go to rehab, but in truth had little choice as she was still under a BA (Baker Act) 52 restraint order, which the psychiatrist had refused to lift, deeming her a suicidal threat.

"Take a look at the person sitting to your right and then to your left," the counselor said. After the audience obliged, she continued in a monotone, "Of the three of you, only one is going to make it."

Now there were some sobering odds, I thought. More statistics ensued as her voice droned on but with a definite air of authority. I tried to figure her out. Medium-build and thin, she had leathered skin and brown hair with blonde streaks. She looked to be sixty, but could have just as easily been forty. I pegged her as a smoker and a recovering alcoholic or addict. The room smelled of stale tobacco and burnt coffee.

"There are now over nineteen-thousand alcohol-induced deaths in the United States each year, and this does not include motor vehicle fatalities."

"There are over twenty-five thousand deaths in the United States from Chronic Liver Disease and Cirrhosis."

"Alcohol is involved in at least fifty percent of all driving fatalities."

"In the United States, every thirty minutes, someone is killed in an alcohol-related traffic accident."

"Over fifteen million Americans are dependent on alcohol, and five-hundred thousand are between the ages of nine and twelve."

"Forty-three percent of Americans have been exposed to alcoholism in their families."

As I listened to her lecture, I sat there transfixed, in a state of shock and disbelief. It was the face of denial again. *This is a mistake. I will awaken shortly from a bad dream. Not me. Not my wife. Not the love of my life, etc,* I thought. *She will stop drinking, her liver will recover, and we will all go back to being a happy and loving family again.* Staring with no outward emotion at the woman with the raspy smokers' voice, I sat mesmerized—paralyzed by the evil twins of fear and anger.

I glanced over at Tina, who seemed to be locked onto the counselor's lecture as if she was reciting gospel. I could not tell if any of this was sinking in or not. She appeared to be hanging onto every word out of the woman's mouth. My head throbbed and my mind spun like a whirling dervish. I could not think about work or myself now. Rather, I was focused entirely on Tina's recovery, and how she was going to get "fixed." Looking around the room, I thought, "*What a bunch of losers—addicts and drunks.*" I heard lots of phrases and buzzwords like "Easy does it," "First things first," and "Keep it simple," but as a newbie, they held no meaning for me.

Having seen these phrases on people's car bumpers, I'd never known what they meant, but I was about to find out soon. There were also plenty of pamphlets, with disturbing titles, like "Al-Anon is For Men Too," and "So You Love an Alcoholic." Soon the intake session was over, and I was ushered out of the sterile building for lock-down. Giving Tina a perfunctory kiss goodbye, I felt relieved, and quickly exited.

"*At least she won't be walking out of here any time soon,*" I said, talking to myself in the parking lot. I never gave a thought to the fact that she could fail this treatment. Despite the odds against her, I concluded that our love and beautiful daughter would save her, for no sane person could throw this away.

Driving home with my stomach in knots, I felt alternating waves of hunger and nausea. With my mother at home helping me with Emily, I could not help but think of my innocent rural upbringing in Middletown, New York, a small town in the rolling jade green hills of apple and dairy country.

"*Why me?*" I asked myself again, full of self-pity. Later that night, sleeping in fits and starts, I awakened just before dawn in a cold sweat, dreaming of Tina's bloodied body in a train crash.

"So," I said to her the next day at the treatment center, "How's it going?"

"Fine, I guess but…" Tina stammered.

"But what?"

"This place gives me the creeps. There are some real sickos here and I am tired of hearing everyone's tales of woe."

"Oh, I see. You still think you're better, or different from everyone else here, do you?"

Silence. I had already met with her counselor who painted a bleak picture of her denial and lack of insight into her disease. Having already picked up the twelve-step program's lingo, I encouraged her to "*work her program*," and just worry about taking it "*one day at a time.*"

"I just want to go home and see my baby girl!" she sobbed, grabbing my arm. "You've got to sign me out of here before I lose my mind."

"You will. It just won't be for a few more weeks. At least not until you're better."

"No!" she screamed, "This is bullshit! I want to go home now!"

I immediately stood up.

"No. And this meeting is over."

My face burned, my pulse quickened, and I felt my head might explode off my shoulders like an agitated can of soda pop. I could barely find the way to the door. I rang the bell to get out quickly, and with her still shrieking in the background, the buzzer sounded, releasing the latch on the heavy metal frame, and I was able to escape. The sound of her screams followed me all the way out as they bounced off the cold, hard institutional tile floor.

"*God,*" I thought, "*I could really use a drink.*" It was only noon.

"David," my mother asked, "How about hiring someone full-time to help you with Emily?" She was folding laundry in her usual hurried fashion.

"That's a thought. But let's just see how the next few weeks go please. My partners have let me off of night call, so I'm okay that way. Besides, Emily's in school during the day. However, I will give it serious thought."

As she continued to fold, and not even make eye contact with me, she said, "When you were a small boy, I raised all of you kids and worked full-time as well. It was exhausting, but I did it because I had to. Your father, may he rest in peace, was a better doctor than a parent. I don't want to see your career suffer when help for your daughter can be arranged. Your work is hard enough without having to raise a child by yourself as well."

"Mom, she may get better."

Finally looking at me with a sympathetic smile, as only a mother can, she said just one word.

"Perhaps."

With Tina's discharge from rehab imminent, I had taken my mother's advice, and hired a full time nanny. Toni was a large middle-aged woman who had only known child rearing her whole life. A simple woman of Romanian descent, she was hard working and liked to cook and clean. Her references were impeccable and I felt that I'd at last caught a break.

Emily immediately liked her, but didn't understand why her mother still wasn't home yet. When she visited her at rehab, all Tina would do is cry, and I didn't think that was healthy. I went to family meetings and couple's counseling with some reluctance. In one week she would be released, and in truth, I was terrified. In preparation, at home I cleaned out all of my beer and wine from the fridge, and had locks installed on my three hundred bottle antique wine cabinet. I removed a poster of the last Sarasota Food & Wine Festival we had attended, and even threw away my binder of wine labels I had collected. As I flipped through the pages, an overwhelming sense of gloom and remorse overtook me. There were comments about where we had drunk the wine, and what food we had with it, and who had been at dinner. I realized again that my life was now unalterably changed—a chapter closed forever.

Walking out of the Fairwinds rehab center in Clearwater, it was a cold but sunny February day, at least by Florida standards. Hugging all of her new recovering alcoholic "friends" good-bye, they promised to stay in touch. Emily was at home with Toni, and I introduced Tina to her. Tina viewed her with detached suspicion and veiled contempt, however, voiced little objection. Toni hung around for a few hours, finishing up some laundry, but when Tina sat on the floor, playing Chutes and Ladders with Emily, she left, and the Mokotoff family was reunited again.

"Can I fix some meals?" she asked.

"Of course."

With trepidation, she opened the refrigerator, and for the first time in her life, there were no beverages inside which contained alcohol. Reaching for one of the many bottles of San Pellegrino sparkling water, she poured herself a tall glass, and sipped. Slowly she turned to me and said simply, "I am so very sorry."

She had lost over ten pounds in one month but looked a lot healthier. Her belly was smaller, her ankles slimmer, and her yellow sclera were almost white again. The first night was icy. Both of us felt as if there was a wall dividing the bed, and neither Tina nor I wanted to reach out to the other. Without the ever-present alcohol to grease her social wheels, she was a fish out of water. In over twenty years, she had never gone this long without a drink. Crying softly in her pillow, I reached over to her shoulder, held her and we kissed. We did not make love—I wasn't even sure who she was anymore.

At first she went to an AA meeting everyday with her goal being "Ninety/Ninety." In AA lingo that was short for "ninety meetings in ninety days," a desirable post-discharge goal from any twenty-eight day rehab program. It was viewed as one of the best ways to maintain sobriety and re-enter the non-drug world. I cooked most of the meals, but she gradually found her way back to the kitchen. Her days were filled with doctors' appointments, AA meetings, reading the "big blue book," otherwise known as the "AA Bible," and resting. One week later we made our first complete meal together—schezuan chicken, pasta pancakes, and roasted vegetables. As I swirled the cooked angel hair pasta with oil and soy sauce in a large stainless steel bowl and gently slid it into a lightly oiled cast iron fry pan, the aromatic sizzle and smoke filled the kitchen. I hit the fan over the stove and turned to her as she was placing root vegetables into the oven.

"It's nice to have you back again," I said.

Her eyes went down, her shoulders slumped a bit, and then she lifted her head. Her eyes were moist, and she only said, "Thanks."

After putting Emily to bed, we stayed up and watched a movie, then enjoyed a hot bubble bath together in our large cream-colored Jacuzzi tub. As I washed her back, my arms encircled her. I kissed the nape of her neck and she hummed. Pivoting, she mounted me in the tub. As we sank into each other's arms, I thought, *This is the woman I fell in love with.* That night, I slept better than I had in months.

Slip

Tina didn't make her ninety-day goal—in fact, she barely had one month of sobriety. By now, I had come to know the signs all too well: less cooking, incoherent speech, and late for appointments. With a nanny around, it was easier for her to slip up since she had fewer responsibilities. I again refused to accept the obvious until Toni called me one morning at work—something she had never done before.

"I'm very sorry to disturb you Dr. David, but I do not think I can work here anymore. I love your daughter—like my own. But your wife is still sick and she talks badly to me."

"Can you tell me how?"

"She tells me I am lousy cook, and fat, and that Emily is her daughter and not mine. She make me feel not so good—no employer ever talk to me like this before. I am good and honest worker."

"I'm sorry. I will speak with her, of course. Is there anything I can do to have you stay?"

"No. But I will stay one more week until you find other help."

"You didn't answer the phone today," I said to Tina when I came home from work that day.

"I was taking a nap," she said. My suspicions were rising. "Where is Emily?" I asked looking around.

"She's next door with Samantha," she said.

"Are you okay?"

"Of course, silly. Why wouldn't I be?"

My mind started to click like a computer. There was so much at stake—so much for her to lose. No way. She's been dry for almost a month—after all she has put us through, she couldn't be drinking again.

"I'll be right back," I said. Without saying another word to her, I stomped out the door into the cool, but moist, winter air. It felt like rain was coming and then another Florida cold front which would bring dry crisp conditions—at least for one to two days. The cul-de-sac was quiet except for the shrieks of Emily and Samantha splashing in the solar-heated pool in the Staub's backyard. I rang the front doorbell and waited.

"Hi" Eileen said.

"I just wanted to know if everything was okay with Emily being here."

"No problem. We love her like our own. She and Sam play like sisters. They're in the pool with the dogs. Won't you please come in?"

I stepped into the foyer where a large antique grandfather clock was banging out six chimes. There was an uncomfortable lull in the conversation. My stomach was starting to knot and my whole body perspired. My throat went dry.

"May I have some water?"

"Sure. Are you all right?"

My mind started to race with fear as she returned with the tall glass of water and crushed ice.

"You don't look well. Why don't you come in and sit down?"

"Is Dan home?" I asked about her husband. "I'm not disturbing your dinner, am I?"

"Heavens no," she said and laughed. "He's working late."

Eileen was a slender dark-haired and black-eyed beauty from Atlanta. She had lost her drawl a long time ago, but still had the genteel manners of a southern woman. Her family had known everything about Tina's drinking from the first hospitalization to the rehab stint a month ago.

As I sat down, I finally let it out.

"Maybe it's my imagination, but I am concerned that Tina may be drinking again. Have you noticed anything different about her lately?"

"No. Not really. But I haven't seen her much the past few days. We've talked on the phone of course, but we used to go out shopping quite a bit. However, with the shows coming up, I've been real busy."

Eileen and Dan raised Portuguese Water show dogs, and the AKC show circuit was about to begin. To me the dogs looked like a cross between a French poodle and a Bouvier des Flandres. Two of the dogs were swimming in the pool with the girls. A third one came in and started to sniff me. I extended the back of my hand with fingers curled down in a non-threatening approach that he accepted. Only then did he allow me to pet his head. His coat was still wet but it didn't exude the usual "wet dog" scent.

"He likes you," Eileen said, trying to make me more comfortable.

"Okay," I said, "it's probably nothing."

"I'll keep an eye out for her and let you know if something looks suspicious, okay?"

"Sure. Thanks."

As I got up to get Emily, I could see her and Samantha playing with their American Girl dolls out by the pool. The dogs were still frolicking in the water, spraying up small waves on the girls as they giggled.

"It's time to go home," I said, swooping up her still wet body in my arms.

"Where are we going for dinner?" she asked.

"Where would you like to go?"

"Big Daddy's Pizza!" she squealed.

"Oh no. Not again!" I groaned.

"Please, please, please," she persisted.

"Okay."

I towel dried her off, and after a hurried good-bye, we walked across the street, hands clasped. More perceptive than I had ever noticed before, she asked me something as if reading my mind.

"Daddy, is mommy sick again?"

The three of us went to dinner. Tina was subdued and quiet. It was as if only Emily and I were at the table. Tina sipped diet Coke while Emily and I talked about her pre-school and what summer camps she might attend. Tina, usually talkative, looked both agitated and distant. I noticed that her face was again puffy, and her eyes were bloodshot. The obvious could no longer be ignored, but I did not want to make a public scene in front of Emily.

"You're not eating your pizza," I said to Tina.

"I'm not hungry," she said. Seal was singing, "Kiss from a Rose" on the piped-in music.

"You don't look so good. How do you feel?" I asked.

"I'm fine!" She yelled, slamming her soft drink on the table as she folded her arms and stared at me in defiance.

"Okay, okay," I answered. "I'm just worried about you. I wasn't trying to start a fight."

She just sat and fumed as Emily and I finished our meal. I asked for a check, left some cash and we went home. I bathed Emily and put her to bed, as Tina stared blankly at the family room television—silent.

In bed later, I tried one more time.

"Do you want to talk about it?" I asked her.

"No," was her only answer. She turned over on side, faced away from me and soon was asleep.

The next day was Saturday and I was on-call for the first time in months. Around noon my pager buzzed on my hip, as I was writing a note in a patient's chart.

"Dr. Mokotoff, please call Eileen Staub at 727-523-1512. She said it was personal." The phone number was for my house.

Why was she calling me from there? Reaching for the nearest phone, I punched in the number.

"David, I'm sorry to bother you at work. First, Emily came over here by herself and she is safe. Tina is at home and she wouldn't answer the phone. So I walked next door. Both the front and back doors were open, and...well...I decided to go inside...I'm afraid that you were correct. She's passed out cold and I can't rouse her."

"Is she breathing?"

"Yes, and snoring."

"Then most likely she's just drunk. Any bottles around?"

"None that I can see."

"Okay. Stay with her please. I will be there as soon as I can. I'm leaving the hospital now."

I thought to myself, Oh no, not again!

Half-dragging and half-carrying her into the rehab center, I had the instant desire to dump her off on the front step with just one suitcase and a note, "Please fix and do not return until sober."

It seemed like only yesterday that we had left Fairwinds—not two months ago. Most of the counselors were recovering addicts and alcoholics themselves, now with degrees in psychiatric social work or psychology, the logic being that they could relate better to their patients than a clean and sober person.

After signing all the obligatory forms, I waited for an intake, or admissions counselor, and then remembered my days at summer camp. So this was the reward for her addiction? She gets unlimited psychotherapy, no parental responsibilities, and three meals and two desserts a day. All she had to do was her laundry, make her bed, and go to meetings. In other words, just show up. There was no final exam or expectations to graduate. You didn't have to even listen and you certainly did not need to talk. What a deal! I thought.

Meanwhile, I had to go home and pick up the pieces of destruction left in her wake again. There would be dirty laundry and new bills from her latest shopping sprees while intoxicated. I would have go to work—save lives—and then explain to my daughter how Mommy had screwed up again. Oh yeah, and find a new nanny. The walls and floor seemed to be closing in on me.

"Hello. I'm Beth," the counselor said, extending her hand. "May I speak with you privately?"

"Of course," I answered, as another staff member whisked Tina away for her initial exam. Entering the small consultation room, I could not help but notice the current residents milling about the television lounge. If they did not have a coffee cup in their hand, it was a cigarette, or both. Having gone to dozens of Al-Anon meetings, the plethora of AA slogans on the wall was by now all too familiar— I could recite them in my sleep.

"I am guessing that this may not be easy for you," Beth said, after closing the door. The room smelled musty.

"Your guess is correct," I said, annoyed. I started to fidget in my chair.

"This may be difficult for you to accept, but most alcoholics are in far more pain than we can ever know."

"How can that be if they're always drunk?" I shot back, not sparing a drop of sarcasm. As soon as the words left my lips, I regretted saying them.

"I'm sorry. I'm very bitter and angry right now. Here's the thing— she has everything a woman could want, a loving husband, beautiful daughter, and money. Why is she so unhappy?"

"Those are all wonderful things, yes. But what she doesn't have is inner peace. Her mind is tormented. I'm sure that you know about her past?"

"Yes," I said at first without thinking much about the question. A second later, I amended my answer.

"You mean about her poor upbringing and alcoholic stepfather?"

Her face showed no expression. "Not just that. I mean the abuse. She has told you about that she hasn't she?"

"She told me that she was raped by her stepfather when she was young, but I never knew for certain if it was true."

I could see a serious frown forming. "In my experience, this is the kind of incident not attributable to fantasy. Have you ever spoken with any of her sisters about this?"

"No," I said. "Do you think I should?"

"If you feel comfortable confiding in them, yes. Have any of them reached out to you?"

I acknowledged that they had. In fact, her mother and sisters had called me often for updates on her condition. I could not bring myself to discuss Tina's past with Helen, but I was certain some of her sisters would help.

"She just never made a big deal about this. I thought she was over it by now."

Her frown slowly turned into a soft smile as she said, "A person is never over something like this. She's in denial about it. The alcohol is how she is dealing with it. You can see how well that has worked can't you?"

I knew then I too was still in denial, and perhaps my marriage hung upon the admission and exploration of her traumatic past. I nodded my head.

"We'll try and work on those issues again in group and private therapy. This is tricky, and let me be the first to tell you how sorry I am. If it is any comfort to you, most alcoholics fail at least two or three times before they find prolonged sobriety."

"My marriage won't last that long," I uttered.

Driving away from the rehab center, self-absorbed and befuddled, my thoughts turned dark—I can't do this again. It's asking too much of me. She will never be well.

Out of nowhere, a large Range Rover cut in front of me. I slammed on the breaks and pressed on the horn. Narrowly missing the guy's tailgate, my Lexus swerved to the right. As I fought to control the wheel, my tires caught the muddy drop off by the asphalt. As I looked in horror, a large oak tree loomed. I pumped my foot repeatedly and stopped at the base of the tree, just before ramming it. Exploding out of my buckle and seat, I raised my fist to the now disappearing SUV.

"Asshole!" Shaking, I slumped back into the car. I started to cry uncontrollably and pounded the dashboard with my fists. My beeper buzzed and I tried to ignore it, but the incessant beeping left me no choice but to look at it. It was a "stat" page from the emergency room.

"Crap!" was the only thing I could say.

Interlude

Sitting in my car, I took a deep breath before responding to my beeper. A medical emergency was the last thing I wanted to handle after just readmitting Tina to the rehab center, but I was on call and someone needed my help.

"We've got a forty-nine year man with no previous cardiac history and severe chest pains. His ST segments (referring to his electrocardiogram) are way up—I think he's having an anterior wall MI (heart attack)." The calm voice on the other end of the phone was Cathy Phillips, a proficient ER doc I had known for over a decade.

"How far away are you?" she asked.

"Up in Clearwater, but I can be probably be there in about twenty minutes. Does he have any contraindications for thrombolytic therapy?"

In 1995, coronary stents for heart attacks were not used routinely as they are today. Instead, we gave powerful "clot-busting" drugs, called thrombolytics, to patients in the early stages of a heart attack to dissolve the blood clot in the artery and restore normal blood flow. It was about ninety percent effective.

"None," she answered. "Do you want me to start the t-PA protocol?"

Normally I would like to see the electrocardiogram first to confirm the diagnosis, but being nowhere near a fax machine, I was just going to have to trust her. We have a saying in cardiology—"Time is muscle"—meaning the sooner you unclog the artery, the more heart muscle and permanent damage you prevent.

"Yes," I answered with little hesitation.

A half-hour later, I was glad I had made that decision. The middle-aged man's electrocardiogram had returned to normal and his pain was completely gone. It had worked like magic. The irony of the event did not escape me. This man's heart attack was stopped in its tracks and cured. Yet, my wife's alcoholism had eluded thousands of dollars and hours of psychotherapy and rehabilitation.

During her first stint in rehab I was an obedient and loyal husband. I would attend Al-Anon meetings several times a week and visit Tina for family and group counseling sessions every weekend. The group sessions were much like an AA meeting and always opened with *"The Serenity Prayer."*

"God grant me the serenity
To accept the things I can not change,
Courage to change the things I can,
And the wisdom to know the difference."

Then a leader would start on a topic, like guilt, anger, relapses, etc, and those attending would chime in with their own personal experiences and opinions. At first I would just sit quietly and listen. However, after a while I did start to share my feelings of doubt and frustrations.

"I don't understand why they can't just stop drinking?" I asked.

Family members of the alcoholics and addicts would nod their head in silent agreement and some would just smile.

It was explained to me that alcoholism was a disease, much like diabetes or cancer, and therefore could not be cured—a position and analogy which I never entirely believed. What the group meetings would do for me however was to free me of any sense of guilt or responsibility for her illness.

Catch phrases and sayings like "The Three C's" made dealing with the alcoholic easier. In referring to the addiction, no one "caused it," nor could it be "cured" or "controlled." This shifted the responsibility for sobriety squarely upon the shoulders of the alcoholic and not their friends or families.

One on one therapy was between Tina and her counselor. I was not involved in these meetings, since again the goal of sobriety could only be attained through her and not me.

Her family, despite all of their dysfunction and alcohol abuse seemed clueless.

"I don't understand why she can't stop," her sister Sue said to me during this time of relapsed rehab. "Doesn't she know what she is risking if she doesn't stop?"

I would give back standard AA answers, but since almost none of them were active in AA or Al-Anon, it was akin to explaining calculus when you have not learnt the times table first.

"You're going to lose David and Emily," Meighan said to her in rehab. Tina would shrug, acknowledge the obvious, and then change the subject.

"We are here to see Tina Mokotoff," I told the receptionist. Emily, wearing an expensive Oilily dress her mother had bought her, held my hand tight. In her other hand, she carried a bouquet of fresh cut flowers. I had pulled her long curly hair back inside a twisted rubber band with plastic balls, the only way I knew to fix it.

A week had passed, and I hadn't visited or called Tina. Hurt and angry, I took her relapse as a personal affront. Her mother and several sisters visited her that first week but privately expressed to me their frustration with her too. I had hired a new nanny, gone to Al-Anon meetings almost every night, and felt ready to go back to work. The weekend was looming and I wanted to take Emily for a visit, but feared my own hostility. Sunday was family day at rehab, where family meetings and counseling sessions were encouraged. However, this time I refused to attend—I went so Emily could see her mother and that was it. I did not want anymore talking or therapy—I wanted to see results and soon.

My heart skipped a few beats when she appeared in jeans and a J. Crew long sleeve t-shirt. Her hair was down, wavy, and freshly washed. She looked thin and remorseful, much like a dog with its head down and tail between its legs.

"Mommieeee!" Emily shrieked. Tina bent down and scooped her up and hugged her like she would never let go. As tears streamed down both of their faces, my anger started to ebb. They went into the sun-drenched cafeteria and sat near the meditation garden. I sat silently while she and Emily talked about school, pets and new foods Emily had just learned to like. As I gazed out at the white cement Buddha sculpture surrounded by hibiscus and lush bougainvillea plants, I felt frozen to the chair. Emily asked if she could go out to the bushes and flowers and look for butterflies. Tina nodded and Emily scampered out.

"I know that you're disappointed in me. I want you to know that I am trying," Tina said, her lips quivering.

"Trying won't cut it anymore. If you keep drinking, you'll be dead. What I don't get is how can you throw away everything you have—a beautiful daughter, a husband who loves you, a nice home, and a great life."

She stared at Emily's half eaten piece of chocolate cake and poked at it with a plastic fork.

"I'm not making excuses, but I was raped when I was twelve. I was denied basic food, clothes, and shelter while my stepfather stuffed his face and drank. I watched him tease and touch my sisters and beat up my grandmother. I can't erase those memories. I can't quiet my mind."

"So you think by staying drunk you will fix it?"

"Addiction doesn't involve thinking, it just makes the thinking stop."

"Well, if you can't stay sober, you won't have a husband or daughter much longer."

"Is that a threat?"

"No. It's a promise. This meeting is over."

And with that I stood up defiantly and went outside.

"It's time to go sweetie," I said to Emily.

"But Daddy, I haven't caught any butterflies yet," she protested.

"Next time. I have to get to the grocery store, and a new nanny is coming over later."

"I don't want another nanny. I want mommy! When is she coming home?"

"Soon...just not today."

Tina and Emily hugged as more tears fell.

Returning from her second stint in rehab, Tina was more sullen and guarded than the last time. Peachy, our latest nanny was a lovely gray-haired woman whose husband had died; her children had stayed up north when their parents had moved to Florida. She drove an old Ford Taurus with 90,000 miles on the odometer, had good references and was an adequate cook. I prayed that Tina wouldn't chase this one away, and at first she reluctantly accepted the nanny's presence with quiet politeness. At other times, she would pretend she wasn't even in the room, or simply didn't exist.

"I will be home late tomorrow," I said to Tina and Peachy at dinner. "I have several cardiac caths in the morning and a dinner meeting tomorrow evening."

"We'll manage just fine," Peachy said as Tina sat expressionless.

"I have to make some phone calls and then will be going to bed early," I said to them both, although it appeared that only the older woman was listening.

I called the hospital to check on some patients and then showered. As I was toweling off, Tina came into the bathroom, and looked like she wanted to talk.

"What's up?" I asked.

"I just wanted to say again how sorry I am. I would like to tell you it won't happen again, but I know you have no reason to believe me." My heart started to soften. This was what I had been seeking—truth and vulnerability. No more lies and denials. I walked to her, and surrounded her with my arms. I turned my head a bit and rested my chin on her shoulder, inhaled her scent—absorbing her shame and fear.

"I love you," I said. "I just want you to get well. If I am cold and distant and angry, it's because I am scared. That's all." As we kissed, she gently dropped her robe to the floor, and led me by the hand to the bed, where we made hurried but passionate love for the first time in weeks.

The period following rehab, when the alcoholic thinks they have their problem beaten, is known as the pink cloud. Overconfidence sows the seeds for disappointment, for no alcoholic truly beats his or her illness. Requiring a conscious decision every day not to drink, the illness demands a true awareness that they are vulnerable at any point in time. And for Tina, she wasn't just floating on the cloud—she was immersed in it.

"Ninety days and ninety meetings," Tina announced one night at dinner.

"Congratulations" I said. "Let's have a toast."

We all raised our glasses of sparking water in the air and touched them together.

"So I guess we won't need your services anymore, Peachy," Tina said suddenly.

Glancing at me for confirmation of the firing or support, I felt my stomach sinking, having been blindsided again. I avoided the nanny's surprised stare.

"Actually, we haven't discussed that yet," I stammered.

However, Tina would not let it go.

"What's there to talk about? I've done everything you've asked of me—I have a sponsor, gone to ninety meetings, and been sober for three months. Why do I need help with my daughter?" she protested.

Fumbling to think of a graceful way out of the quagmire, I turned to her and said, "Yes you have. But this is not just your decision to make. We will talk about it later."

Shoving back from the table, she threw her napkin on her plate, saying only, "Fine! As usual it will be whatever King David wants!"

As she left in a huff, all I could do was look at Emily and Peachy and say, "Well, never a dull moment, here, is there?"

They call them chips—funny little pieces of metal or plastic coins, awarded to the alcoholic by friends and sponsors in the program to award certain milestones of sobriety, like thirty days, ninety days, one year, etc. Each chip is a different color. Approaching her one-year anniversary of sobriety, Tina's cravings were gone. We seemed to have settled into a normal routine, Peachy having been let go. I would go to work, and Tina would take Emily to school, go shopping, a meeting and work out, and then home to watch the soap operas, which her grandmother had called, "The Stories." She would then take Emily to dance lessons and finally home to cook dinner. She needed to keep busy, leaving little time for thinking. She repeated to me more than once the theory that "idleness is the devil's workshop."

Some nights we rented movies from Blockbuster. I will never forget watching one of these with Tina. "Rush" was made in 1991 and starred Jason Patric and Jennifer Jason Leigh as undercover narcotics agents who become lovers when they partner up to infiltrate the Texas drug scene and bring down a suspected drug lord. But as their relationship intensifies, and they become increasingly dependent on each other, they have difficulty resisting the temptations of the world they're trying to subvert. During one of the scenes the female undercover cop "shoots up" with heroin. In explicit fashion, we are shown her tying a tourniquet on one arm, stabbing at a vein in her elbow area with a needle, withdrawing bright red blood, and then injecting the illicit liquid. Her head and eyes roll back as she falls to the floor.

"I can't watch this," Tina said as she stood up to leave the room.

Her being a nurse, this reaction surprised me. Surely she had seen and used needles and syringes many times before. Suddenly I got it.

"Jesus, you've shot up before haven't you?" I said.

She said nothing but her face told me the answer. Hitting the pause mode on the machine, I stood up to face her.

"You told me you never used IV drugs before."

She was trapped by the truth again.

"Only once..." she stammered, "when I was in California. I didn't like it."

I wanted to believe her, but by now had given up on the concept that veracity was high on the list of her character attributes.

"Somehow, I don't believe you," I said. "That might explain why you have Hepatitis C."

She didn't deny this or argue.

"I don't want to fight. I'm tired and going to bed," she said. "You can watch the rest of the movie without me."

Head down, she walked to the other side of our house and into the master bedroom. I finished watching the movie detached from the plot. My thoughts darkened as I brooded about the conversation, my denial, and how I had been fooled again.

"Successful day at the mall?" I said the following week. As I stared at the bright and colorful bags lining the family room floor. The names were by now familiar—Nordstrom's and Neiman Marcus. My question was both sarcastic and rhetorical.

"You're not going to start yelling at me again about shopping are you?" she asked. Her hands laid upon both hips with her elbows cocked out in right angles in a defensive posture.

"I think you could show a little restraint perhaps," I said.

"Well, you know Lynn Orns, (one of her shopping buddies), spends much more than I do!"

"I don't care about her. I'm married to you. Look, I don't want to monitor your clothing purchases, but since you've been out of rehab your mall bills have sky-rocketed."

Trying to be coy instead of fractious she took a new tack. She walked over to me with head cocked to one side, and encircled my waist with her arms. I could smell new perfume exuding scents of roses and jasmine.

"Later, after Emily's asleep, we'll take a nice bubble bath, and I will give you a fashion show. How's that sound?" she asked.

My will was weakening.

"And then," she continued, "I will give you a nice oil massage and we can have sessions."

"Sessions" was her unromantic but funny nickname for lovemaking—apparently she had heard it from her grandmother.

Aroused and disarmed, we hugged and kiss. For the moment at least I stepped away from the shopping battle.

Yet it seemed that she had traded one addiction for another— spending even more time at the new International Mall in Tampa. As I watched the bills pour in, I rationalized that it was at least cheaper than more rehab or divorce, especially if it kept her sober. And stay sober she did. Tina became a loving mother and wife again. We went on normal vacations and had friends over for dinner. We even went out to concerts and enjoyed meals with other couples in fine restaurants. My guard was starting to ease, and as months slipped into years, I again flirted with something dangerous—optimism.

Below Bottom

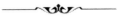

There is a saying in AA that most alcoholics don't find sobriety until they "hit bottom." For some this might be a DUI arrest, or losing a job or spouse. However, there is also another saying—"every bottom has a basement"—meaning just when you think it can't get any worse, it does. For Tina, a series of falls "below bottom" began in March 2001.

We had planned a trip to Big Sky Montana ski resort with friends over the school spring break. Among the friends were Dick Murbach, a cardiothoracic surgeon, his wife Sue and their daughter Chelsea, who was about the same age as Emily. Also going were Beth and Sean Manning, whose son, Sean William, was a classmate of Emily's. This was Dick's second wife, and he had two older daughters from a previous marriage. Having referred him many open-heart surgery patients over the years, he had been generous with me during several vacations, paying for meals and a boat trip to South Seas Plantation Resort on Captiva Island in 1986. On this ski trip, one night he invited us out to dinner at The Rainbow Ranch Restaurant and Bar, in Gallatin, Montana, a couple of miles from the Big Sky Ski resort. Three other couples and children were also invited.

We sat down at a large wooden table, adorned with a white tablecloth and napkins. I could not help but notice the beautiful water and wine goblets, probably Reidel, or some other expensive brand of crystal. A fire was crackling by the wall making the room warm enough to remove several layers of outerwear, and burnt hickory wood aromas abounded. Dick and Sue were well aware of Tina's alcoholism, brush with death in 1995, and her continued sobriety. Thus, it was not a surprise when he asked me just before the meal, "Is it okay if I order a couple bottles of wine for the table?"

With six years of my wife's sobriety, I did not hesitate to answer.

"Of course not—please—go ahead. We'll be okay."

Tina and I had gradually grown used to this routine. If someone else ordered wine and offered, I would have a glass or two, and she would stick with sparkling water. In fact, after the wine order was placed on such occasions, she would ceremoniously turn her wineglass over to avoid the inevitable question from the waiter—"Will you be having wine this evening ma'am?"

That night I sat stunned as she failed to turn over the wineglass. At first I thought it was just a mistake, and I watched with increasing agitation as the waiter began to uncork the bottle of 1999 Duckhorn Three Palms Vineyard Merlot from Napa Valley, California. It had always been one of our favorite red wines. Sitting stone-faced, I stared at the waiter who finally made his way to Tina for the inevitable question. I said nothing. Instead, I felt as if I was watching an unfolding car wreck.

To my horror, she said, "Why, yes. I think I will have a little bit please."

After he poured a few ounces of the ruby red spirit into her glass and moved onto the next diner, I grabbed the sleeve of her beige cashmere sweater and whispered into her ear, "What are you doing?"

She smiled at me and the other guests, and said just two words.

"It's okay."

"No," I said. "It is not okay."

Eluding eye contact with me, she retorted, "I know what I'm doing. Please don't make a scene."

I could only sit fuming as others tried to avoid eye contact with either one of us. Without hurry, she drank the glass with her meal and declined a refill. She ignored me as she chatted with the other women and helped Emily choose her meal, a petite filet of buffalo. However, this time I was not being fooled. After two long trips to the bathroom, I was certain she had stopped at the bar to slam down more alcohol. After the meal ended, she weaved and leaned to the right as I helped her with her long camel wool coat and scarf. As we left the restaurant large flakes of snow poured down from the sky. It had been snowing for several hours and there was already at least a half-foot of the brilliant white blanket coating the cars and the parking lot. Walking to my rented four-wheel drive SUV, our boots made crunching sounds in the still mountain air. Minutes after driving away Emily fell asleep in the back seat. Tina and I said nothing.

By the time we reached our mountainside ski-in ski-out condo, the snow was close to a foot deep. The halogen night light in the parking lot reflected the dense powdery flakes as they continued to fall. As I looked up at the sky, the delicate frozen droplets felt heavy on my face, and I could smell burning aspen wood from fireplaces. My stomach turned and my mind tormented, I could not appreciate the beauty of the scene. Inside our condo, I helped Emily to bed and came back out to the front foyer. Tina was still dressed with her coat, hat, and gloves. Her bloodshot gaze gave away her condition.

"Where are you going?" I asked.

"Out," she said.

"I can see that, but where? It's eleven o'clock."

"I'm going to the Manning's house to shoot pool."

Dumbfounded, I could not believe my ears, and said, "No you're not."

"And why is that?" she challenged.

"Because it's late—and married women just don't go out late at night to shoot pool with a guy!"

My cheating antenna was now activated.

Her arms were crossed and she tried in vain to argue the obvious.

"Oh come on now—Sean and I are just friends."

Richard Sean Manning was a tall muscular man with streaming blond hair. His physical appearance gave rise to the nickname "Fabio," after Fabio Lanzoni, an Italian male fashion model who appeared on the cover of hundreds of romance novels throughout the 1980s and '90s. Sean's long flowing locks of hair were striking. Some friends viewed his marriage to Beth Morean as an improbable pair.

Beth's father, William, (Bill) Morean was one of the founders of Jabil Circuit, Inc. Founded with James Golden in 1966 in Detroit, Michigan, the company is a provider of electronic circuit boards for a diverse group of industries. The name came from the combination of the founders' first names, (James and Bill). William Morean died in 1979, and his son, Bill then became CEO and President of the company. The home office was moved to St. Petersburg, Florida in 1982, where it remains today. It is now the second largest company in the Tampa Bay area, employing 61,000 people in the US and abroad. The company is worth several billion dollars.

How Sean Manning came to be married to the boss's daughter

is curious. An article in the St. Petersburg Times recounted some of it in an interview. Born Richard Sean Manning in upstate New York, as a young man he said one day he closed his eyes and placed a finger on a map of the US. It pointed to St. Petersburg, Florida. With little money, he drove down to Florida in his car, which he lived out of for some time, and took a job as a janitor at Jabil's main office building. That is where he met Beth Morean, the President and CEO's sister, whom he eventually married.

Beth was, and still is, a generous, unpretentious and out-going woman. Some friends and acquaintances quietly speculated their marriage was more about money than love. Ever believing in the essential goodness of people, I remained skeptical of this; however, rumors of his affairs with other women were not infrequent. They had two children, but in the end gossip of Sean as a male "gold-digger" were strengthened when they divorced on January 24, 2005.

Today Sean divides his time between St. Petersburg and Cambria, New York running Freedom Winery with his brothers, Larry and Chip. Cambria, only 18 miles from Niagara Falls, is where Sean and his brothers grew up. In St. Petersburg he runs the Sean Manning Foundation, Inc.; his personal history is described a bit differently on his website, www.themanningstudios.com.

"Sean is a self made man, an artist, teacher and a philanthropist. He is a son, brother, father, uncle, business partner and to his friends he is known as Sean. After moving to Florida in 1984 he began working at Jabil Circuit and in no time climbed the ladder into management. He advanced as manufacturing manager and moved to Scotland where he and his young family lived for 2 years. In 2002 he retired to immerse himself in his artistic goals, his family business, and to concentrate on his philanthropic pursuits. When in St. Petersburg, Florida Sean is a partner in St. Pete Clay Company, which provides full facilities to a thriving art community, including studio and gallery space and a vast selection of kilns."

Beth's after divorce endeavors were no less impressive. In an article in the St. Petersburg Times, August 15, 2005, it was stated that "Beth, a local philanthropist and longtime supporter of the Arts Center, had given the lead gift for the center's new $20-million building that would be named the Beth Ann Morean Arts Center." Later she help fund the Chihuly Collection on Beach Drive, showcasing many of the works of Dale Chihuly, an internationally famous glass artist. The comprehensive collection of his work is the only one of its kind in the world.

"Friends—yeah—right," I said to Tina. "And that's what I told your nursing supervisor seventeen years ago when we first started dating. So how long have you been sleeping with him?" My anger was rising.

I wasn't sure if she was just too tired or too drunk to argue, but she stripped off her coat, gloves, hat, and strode back to our bedroom in silent defiance.

My suspicions about her having an affair with Sean Manning were now affirmed. I had done, and did, what I always do—denied the obvious. We had hung out with Sean and Beth Manning a lot over the past months, and I sensed that it wasn't because Tina was good friends with Beth, nor was Emily close to her son and classmate, Sean William.

We flew home the next day and the flight from Bozeman, Montana to Tampa, Florida seemed longer than usual. We said almost nothing to each other. I played a Pee Wee Herman movie on a laptop Mac book computer for Emily, and slept most of the way home.

Events continued to worsen. We lived in the prestigious waterfront community of Pasadena Yacht & Country Club. I had purchased the home in 2000 so I could be on the water, buy a boat, and fish more often. Our next-door neighbors were Tom and Sandy Geller. Tom was a real estate developer and owned several franchised locations of "Crabby Bills," an informal but very popular seafood eatery. Short of stature and thin, he was a fun-loving father and husband who would go out of his way to please his wife and children. Sandy was a dark-haired attractive woman who had grown up in St. Petersburg, and enjoyed just being a mother and wife. Later I would discover that she also had a darker side.

The Geller's home was built just after we moved in, and like them, it was larger than life—three floors with an elevator, huge salt-water aquarium in the front foyer, and an enormous kitchen replete with a gigantic Viking gas range and stove combination, industrial appliances, and copper pots and pans hanging from a suspended ceiling rack. Sandy was a good cook. She also liked to drink.

It didn't take long for Tina to start hanging out with her new "best friend." Since neither one had nine to five jobs, there was plenty of time to schmooze and booze.

One Friday evening in 2002, Tommy invited us to dinner at his Crabby Bill's restaurant on St. Pete Beach. Although the food was mediocre, the view was awesome. Built right on the beach, the expansive windows gave a non-ending view of the Gulf of Mexico. The motif at all of the Crabby Bill's was wooden picnic type tables and benches. There the patrons would hammer out crab claws as pieces of meat and shell would go flying, drink lots of beer and wine, and finish with Key Lime pie.

My "falling off of her wagon" awareness was on high alert already, and I ordered water only with dinner. I thought Tina had done the same. She and Emily ate fish and chips, but by the end of the meal Tina seemed buzzed. I was puzzled.

"I'm tired," Emily said. "Can we go home?"

"Sure honey," I answered. I thanked our hosts and we left the restaurant together. But as I buckled Emily in the back seat I turned around to find Tina gone. Apparently, my wife had other plans. I did not want to leave Emily in the car alone with the engine running at night in front of a restaurant. I stared at the heavy wooden restaurant door, decorated with a large wooden crab on the handle, waiting for Tina to emerge. After a few minutes, which seemed like an hour, she came bouncing out with a white Styrofoam cup in hand.

"We're so close to Sean and Beth's house. Let's just drop in and visit them," she giggled as she slithered into the front passenger seat.

"I don't think so," I answered.

"Oh you're no fun!" she slurred.

Glancing at the white cup, I quickly grabbed it away from her before she could react.

"No!" she screamed, lunging toward me. Her hand just missed my wrist as her fingers slammed into the steering wheel. "Give me that!"

I had already sniffed and tasted the contents. I knew it well— Vodka. Spilling it out on the curb, neither of us said anything. The short drive home was silent except for Emily who was frightened and sniffling, said to her mother, "Mommy, are you okay?"

Turning her head, she went to pat Emily's leg and missed it. As her hand landed on the carpeted steering column in the middle of the floor, she garbled, "Its okay, honey."

I took Emily out of the car, helped her remove the scrunchy from her ponytail, watched as she brushed her teeth, got into her American Girl collection pajamas, and then pointed her to bed. Lying next to her, I read Shel Silverstein's book, "The Giving Tree," and after finishing it she said, "Mommy's drinking again isn't she?"

I did not mince words.

"Yes, I'm afraid so."

"Is she going to die?" she asked.

"I don't know," I hedged.

Fighting back tears, we hugged. She still clung to her childhood cloth bunny rabbit, "Puffy," and said, "I'm tired. I want to go to sleep. I love you, Daddy. Can you leave the light on for me?"

"Yes. And I love you too," I said kissing her forehead.

"Daddy?" she asked as I started to walk away.

"Yes?"

"Can we have pancakes in the morning?"

"You betcha," I said.

As I walked to the other side of the house where the master bedroom suite was located, I stopped mid way, and went out to the screened in porch over-looking the dark water, my dock, and boat. My high intensity halogen lamp sprayed white light across the rippling water as snook ambushed smaller baitfish attracted to the light. Every few minutes the water would pop, as the sleuth game fish would inhale another meal.

I walked down the spiral black iron staircase to the dock where I always kept a fishing pole, and then lifted a yellow plastic bucket of shrimp suspended in the water. I tried to keep them fresh and available so I could fish whenever I wanted. The larger fish spook easily so I used a slow stealth approach on the dock. After baiting my hook with a large flapping crustacean, I walked back to the seawall and casted out. It took less than a minute for the attacker to grab its prey and then my circle hook sank into its lip. Exploding out of the water, I began to reel in fast, careful to maintain constant pressure on the rod and reel. The captive swam straight to a dock pilling thick with oysters and barnacles.

Before I could pull it away, the line was shredded and the cunning fish had escaped.

Sitting for a few moments, I suddenly turned around to a small voice from above.

"Did you catch her Daddy?" Emily asked.

"No, honey, she broke me off," I said.

Clutching her stuffed bedmate and standing in pink pajamas, she said, "She sounded like a big one."

"I think she was, yes."

"You'll get her tomorrow," she said.

"Maybe," I answered. "It's late. Go back to bed and I'll see you in the morning."

"Okay," she answered shuffling back inside.

Entering our bedroom, I saw Tina was passed out in bed, snoring. I showered, grabbed a Carl Hiassen novel, and went to the family room sofa. After reading only three pages, I fell into a deep sleep.

Roller Coaster

The sound of coffee grinding in the kitchen awakened me from an uncomfortable sleep. Emily was in the family room watching cartoons on the Nickelodeon channel. The smell of bacon hit my nostrils as I walked into the kitchen.

Tina was standing there in a plush bathrobe turning blueberry pancakes over.

"Good morning," she said in a sober voice.

"Hello," I grumbled.

"I'm sorry about last night," she said as she offered me a glass of orange juice. As I took it she also shoved a note into my other hand.

I looked at her face and saw a vulnerability that I had not seen in a long time. After sipping my juice, I sat down at the kitchen table, placing the note next to a plate, unopened. As dolphins scooted under my dock chasing mullet, I just stared out at the sparkling water. A crabber in long yellow overalls and black rubber boots was busy lifting one of his crab traps and checking its contents. Small pleasure boats dragging water-skiers and knee-boarders were already racing by in the canal. Tina had the porch door cracked open and the salty humid air was racing in, mixing with the cool air-conditioned spaces.

As she continued to cook and flip bacon and pancakes, she asked me, "Are you ready for coffee?"

"No thanks," I said. "Not just yet."

I opened the note written in her distinctive half cursive, half printed manner. The ink was smudged a bit, but it was succinct and honest.

David,

I know I've said I'm sorry far too many times already, so you have no reason to believe me if I say it again. If I were in your or Emily's place, I wouldn't trust me or my word either. All I can say is that I will keep trying and attempt to do better.

Love,
Tina

I folded the note up then placed it next to a plate, the corner secured from moving.

"Mommy, I'm hungry. Is breakfast ready yet?" Emily said sticking her curly red hair through the doorway.

"Yes. Come on in!"

"Yippy!" she howled.

As we sat silently eating our breakfast with warm maple syrup, I got up to grab myself some coffee. My mind was racing with opposing thoughts. *I should cut my losses and just divorce her now. I love her so much and I don't want to get divorced again. I can't do this to Emily.*

We all avoided any discussion of last evening's events, and I decided to change the topic.

"How about we make a picnic lunch and go out to Shell Island today?"

"Can we look for sand fleas and crabs?" Emily asked.

"Yes," I said.

Tina looked demurred but agreed to go with us. Known once as a small family spot, this spoil island near St. Pete Beach, had been taken over by a younger crowd more interested in partying and booze, and I reflected further on my suggestion.

"Did you have something else in mind?" I asked Tina.

"I need to go to a meeting and call my sponsor," she answered.

"Yes. Of course."

Turning my head to Emily, I said, "How about we just go tubing instead?"

"Can I invite a friend?" she asked.

I nodded my approval.

A plan was in place—at least for a few hours. I had learned that when living with an alcoholic that is pretty much all you can plan for anyway.

Tina waved to us as I pulled the boat out from the lift with three little girls ensconced in bright orange life vests. When we reached the middle of the canal, I attached a large yellow and blue inflatable tube into the water by clamping a stainless steel caribiner device to a towrope and then the boat. As the three girls grabbed the hard rubber handles, they gave me the thumbs up. I put the boat in forward gear and we raced off. Their hair flailed in the salty spray as they hooted and howled. I made several narrow turns over-running my wake, which caused the tube to bounce into the air. As the girls screamed louder I made faster and smaller turns until the tube flipped and all three entered the water. Slowing the boat I carefully approached them, deployed the rear ladder and they climb aboard. We repeated this for about an hour until I finally grew tired.

"Okay. That's it. Let's go home," I said.

"No!" They all shrieked.

"You can go swimming in the pool, then we can all go out for pizza—how's that sound?" I said.

The no's quickly became yes's.

Approaching my dock at low speed, I noticed a dark gray lump in the water near one of my pilings. As a whiskered snout broke the surface, the identity of the creature was revealed.

"Girls, be quiet. It's a manatee," I said in a soft voice.

They all hushed and followed my pointing finger to the large blob feeding on some sea grass. Manatees are large, fully aquatic, herbivorous mammals, known as sea cows. These docile creatures are often injured or killed by unsuspecting boaters who don't see them in the water and the propellers scrape across their backs. Many of the survivors can be seen with permanent long scars on its tough leathery back. They are docile and approachable.

"I tell you what," I said to the girls in a muted voice. "I will tie off the boat so I won't scare it. Get off the boat with soft voices and feet. Em—you run inside and ask your mom if she has any lettuce, and bring it down. Okay?"

"What if she's not there?" she whispered.

"Then just look for something large, leafy, and green in the bottom drawer of the fridge," I said.

They all nodded approval with the plan as Emily bolted up the spiral staircase by the pool to the porch and then the kitchen. Meanwhile I turned a water hose on low pressure and cautiously approached the gentle giant. Its snout raised, at first it eyed me with suspicion. When it felt the soft freshwater spray on its face, it turned, mouth open, gulping down the treat. As Emily arrived back at the dock with a large wilted head of Romaine lettuce, I divided the greens amongst the three girls.

"Now don't give it to her all at once," I said.

The large cow, which I estimated to be at least seven feet long, took the vegetable without hesitation, munching in silence. The girls giggled in muted voices.

"Daddy—look—it's a baby!" Emily said.

Sure enough a small blob emerged next to its mother, curious about all of the fuss and action. Emily gave it a drink, and I extended it some salad as well.

"Can we swim with them?" Emily asked.

At first I hesitated, but knowing the non-violent creatures wouldn't harm them, I said, "Okay, but pet them gently, and keep your life vests on."

I watched all three enter the warm water down the dock ladder without hesitation. Emily was the first to approach the mom and she gave it a gentle pat on the back. It nuzzled her like a big St. Bernard. I knew the mammal's back was rough.

"Check out her belly," I said to her.

Taking a gulp of air, she dove down and rubbed its belly.

Emerging to the surface seconds later, she yelled. "It's so soft!"

I nodded. The other girls did the same until we ran out of treats. The mother and child sea cows dove down into the dark muddy bottom, searching for more food, then disappeared.

By the time we all showered and dressed, Tina was gone. I took the girls out for pizza and then a movie. I was tired and it was late afternoon. After dropping the girls back at their homes, I then drove back to the country club. As my car bar code sticker was scanned and a wooden gate lifted, I had a feeling of impending doom. Tina had not answered her mobile or the house phone all afternoon.

Driving into the garage, I saw her beige Mercedes Benz in the garage with a flat rear tire. I became even more suspicious as I climbed the stairs and detected the stench of alcohol.

Emily fed off of my anxiety.

"Where's Mommy?" She asked lips trembling.

"I'm not sure, but I will find her. Please go to your room and wait."

"No. I don't want to—I'm scared—I'm scared—."

I did not wait for her to finish. "Emily—do as I say—go to your room now!"

Entering our master bedroom I was struck by three things. The door to the outside was wide open as heavy and wet air poured in, the television was on and blaring, and Tina was passed out cold on the bed with a gash on her forehead. I tried to rouse her but she didn't respond. Her respirations were long, slow, and labored, her pulse weak and rapid—I called 9-1-1.

After giving them the details, it took only five or ten minutes for the paramedics and ambulance to arrive, sirens and lights screaming. As two EMT persons entered our bedroom, they took her vital signs, which were not good. One of them started an intravenous line and some oxygen while the other radioed St. Anthony's Hospital in St. Petersburg.

"St. Anthony's ER, go ahead," the walkie-talkie cracked.

"Yes, this is St. Pete Fire and Rescue, number seven-eight-six. We are at a residence with a middle-aged female, about forty years old, with apparent alcohol and as yet unknown drug overdose. She has a superficial scalp wound without obvious bleeding. Her respirations are twelve, pulse one hundred and twenty, and blood pressure is eighty over sixty. Do you copy?"

"Yes, rescue seven-eight-six. Establish IV line and okay to transport," a distant and impersonal male voice spoke back.

"We copy," he said. "We'll see you in ten or fifteen minutes."

As soon as her IV line was being strapped in place, Tina woke up and started yelling. Her face was red and bloated, and her speech slurred.

"Who are you and what are you doing to me?" she yelled at the paramedic by her side.

He tried to calm her down. "You passed out and may have a head injury. Please lie still."

She began to buckle without warning and almost ripped out the plastic tubing in the back of her hand. "No! I'm not going anywhere. Where's my baby?"

Squinting from puffy eyes she targeted me, saying, "David, no—don't let them do this!"

I shook my head and said without hesitation, "I can't stop them. This time you've gone too far."

And with that she began to writhe and thrash about even more. It took all of the two men's power to hoist her onto a collapsible gurney and then restrain her with thick brown leather buckles at the chest and legs, arms tightly secured to her side. Powerless she began to spit at them as they moved her from the bedroom to the top of the stairs.

By this point Emily had heard the commotion, come out of her room, and cowered behind a couch. Tina screamed and spat all the way out to the ambulance. Emily finally emerged and grabbed my leg like a vice. I scooped her up in my arms and hugged her as we descended the stairs and out the front door.

By this time several of the neighbors had gathered to view the developing donnybrook until the ambulance pulled away, again with sirens blaring and lights flashing. From the side of my vision, I saw Sandy Geller had come over and started to speak before I could say anything. She looked hammered as well, but at least was coherent.

"I'm sorry," she started. "We only had a couple of drinks this afternoon."

With overt sarcasm, I shot back, "For her that was two drinks too many. Were you over here?"

"Yes. She seemed fine when I left," she answered in a half defensive and fearful voice.

With that I went inside with Emily and plopped her down in front of the living room television. "I need to get something," I said. "I will be going to the hospital. I'm going to call Elisa or Mallory's mom, and see if they can watch you for a few hours. Is that okay?"

She nodded yes.

I went directly to my bathroom medicine cabinet in search of some Xanax, (a medication which was prescribed to me for anxiety a few months back). The bottle had noted thirty pills, and I recalled taking only three or four. There were only two left! I assumed that it was Sandy, Tina, or both, who had popped them.

I quickly called the Posey's house and reached Lisa. John and Lisa Posey lived in the neighborhood with their three girls, Mallory, Madison, and Miranda. Their boat was appropriately named, "The M&M's." John was a stockbroker with Raymond James and Lisa a homemaker. They were solid parents and knew about Tina, loved Emily like one of their daughters, and agreed to take her overnight without hesitation.

"You're going to the Posey's tonight," I said to Emily. "Is that okay?"

"Yes," she said. "But Daddy will you call me later about mommy?"

"Of course I will," I answered. "Now go to your room and pack some pajamas and your toothbrush and I will drop you off there."

As she marched off to her room I thought *she deserves better than this.*

Teresa Bradley was the head emergency doctor that day at St. Anthony's Hospital. I had known her for years and she was a good doc with great clinical judgment. On my ride in my cell phone rang—the caller ID said "St. Anthony's Hospital ER."

"Hello, this is Dr. Mokotoff," I said.

"Please hold for Dr. Bradley," the secretarial voice replied.

After a few moments, she came to the phone.

"Hi David. This is Terry Bradley. I've examined your wife—we did a CT scan of her head and there's no cerebral bleeding. Her drug screen was negative, but her alcohol level was four hundred and fifty seven. Her blood counts are out of whack of course—she'll need to be admitted."

"Okay, thanks. I will be there in a few," I answered.

The negative drug screen ruled out Xanax ingestion but the alcohol level was the highest I had ever seen with Tina, and it alone was alarming. Anything more than eighty was grounds for a DUI in Florida, and a number over four hundred was usually associated with unconsciousness or death.

Tina slept for the next twenty-four hours and was seen by blood and liver specialists and a psychiatrist. They all painted the same bleak picture for me.

"If you drink again, you will die," I said to her two days later after she finally awoke.

Looking disheveled and humble, she just nodded her head.

"So what would you like to do this time?" I asked.

Her silence only agitated me further.

"Well since you're out of ideas, here's mine. You either go to rehab again, or I will ask your psychiatrist to lift your BA 52 (Baker Act for involuntary incarceration due to harm to one's self or others), and you can return home—with daily alcohol breath tests. If you fail even one, I will immediately file for divorce and full custody of Emily." The gauntlet had been thrown down, and a line in the sand drawn.

Her lips began to quiver, tears appeared and her body language was one of defeat. I saw her head and shoulders slump forward.

"I won't go back to rehab again," she said defiant to the end.

"Okay then. You'll probably be released today. Get showered and ready to go."

What she didn't know was that I had already visited a divorce attorney, Steve Thacker, in Clearwater, Florida and had divorce papers ready to file upon my command.

It took her only three days to flunk a Breathalyzer test. Her answer to both Emily and I was incredulous—she had eaten some "old grapes from the refrigerator and they must have been fermented!" She alternated between incapacitated and actually functional. I forbade her from driving Emily anywhere unless she was sober. I rearranged car pools and pulled out all the "IOU's" I could from friends and neighbors to haul Emily to and from school and dance lessons. I even warned the school that Tina was not allowed to pick Emily up at the end of classes.

One afternoon, this plan came to a climax. Tina showed up to the school pick up line intoxicated, and they did not feel comfortable releasing Emily to her care. The administrator's secretary, Diana Craig, had my cell phone number and explained the still evolving confrontation. I was only a few minutes away and raced over, just as the conflict was heating up. Tina's beige Mercedes Benz was pulled off to the side of the line of pick up cars and SUV's. Emily was standing on the school steps holding Diana Craig's hand as Tina berated the secretary.

"She's my daughter—give her to me! You can't keep her here."

"I'm very sorry Mrs. Mokotoff, but we have instructions from your husband not to release her to you," Diana said in a diplomatic tone.

Tina just circled around the secretary and Emily, mumbling expletives. Just as I approached her, a hand tapped my shoulder. It was Wendy Walker. Her daughter, Madeline, and Emily were classmates. Wendy was an evangelical Christian and we had a history of disagreement a few years back when Madeline had told Emily on the playground she would "go to hell" if she did not accept Jesus as her savior. However, this time, Wendy would be my momentary salvation.

"David, can you let me handle this please?"

Not relishing a public scene, and out of ideas, I agreed.

Wendy was tall with shoulder length hair, dressed fashionably but not in a way that screamed money—like most of the mothers at Emily's private school, where fake boobs and huge diamonds all competed against one another for the "richest image." I was relieved and fascinated. *What could they have in common?* I thought.

Wendy's hands were on both of Tina's shoulders. It looked to me as if Tina was about to be baptized. Wendy did most of the talking and Tina nodded her head, slowly went to her car and drove away.

Wendy walked Emily over to me and as I strapped her into my car, I said to her, "We'll go home in a minute. I have to talk to Madeline's mom. Is that okay?"

She nodded as tears poured down her cheeks. I left the air conditioner on and closed the car door. Facing Wendy I said, "I don't know what you told her, but thank you."

Wendy was frank and to the point.

"David, I am a recovering alcoholic. I know where she's at right now. You don't need to thank me. Just take care of Emily and let me know if there is anything else I can do to help."

I gave her a polite hug, slid into the driver's seat and took Emily home.

I made dinner and took Emily to her evening dance lessons. At home Tina was being reclusive but I saw no point in stalling the inevitable.

"I'm filing for divorce tomorrow," I said to her as she sat in the family room, hammered and distant. She just stared at "Entertainment Tonight" on the screen as the bleach-blond "newscaster" gave juicy details of the latest Hollywood celebrity scandal.

"You will receive some money as agreed upon in our pre-nuptial agreement. You can keep the Mercedes, and I will buy you a condo. I want you out of here as soon as possible."

Silence.

"Do you understand what I'm saying?" I asked without sympathy and little emotion.

She nodded her head.

This was my point of "no mas," (Spanish for no more), or "enough." Emily and I could not go on living this way. So no matter what the cost, I now knew what I needed to do. She would either find sobriety—which would be great, or she would die. Either way, I finally let go of the illusion that I had any control, and never had, of her drinking. Her future was in her hands now—I was done. I knew I could be nice or mean to her and it didn't matter. She would drink because she was an alcoholic and well—that's what they do.

"Fine!" she yelled in final defiance.

Slowly rising from the couch, she staggered to the bedroom, found some luggage pieces, and began to pack.

Photo Section

David and Tina Mokotoff at the Abilities Foundation
Wine Tasting Event in St. Petersburg, Florida, March 1994

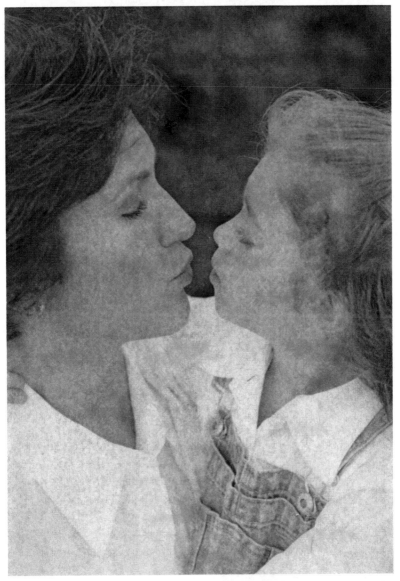

Tina and Emily Mokotoff, 1996

Tina, Emily, and David Mokotoff, December 1998

Lucky and Emily, 1996

David and Emily fishing in
Estes Park, Colorado,
August 1996

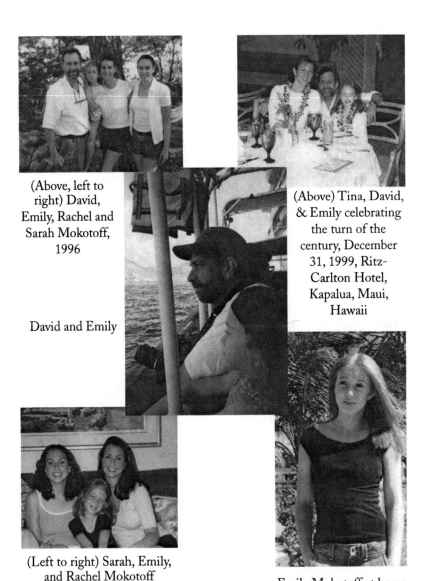

(Above, left to right) David, Emily, Rachel and Sarah Mokotoff, 1996

(Above) Tina, David, & Emily celebrating the turn of the century, December 31, 1999, Ritz-Carlton Hotel, Kapalua, Maui, Hawaii

David and Emily

(Left to right) Sarah, Emily, and Rachel Mokotoff

Emily Mokotoff at home in Gulfport, Florida, 2002

Ackerson family reunion, Ft. De Soto Park, Florida, June 1994
(From top to bottom and left to right.) Jodi, Mary Kim (Penny),
Meighan, Pam, Tina, Sue, Bobby, Bud, X., and Chip

Penny and her father
Bruce "Moose" Ackerson

Tina, Meighan, and Bruce
"Moose" Ackerson at wedding
of Penny and Elliott Weinger,
Turnberry Isle Country Club,
Florida on December 5, 1993

(Right) Bruce "Moose" Ackerson
with daughter Tina, 1955

Jodi Ackerson Lane, and Alexis Lane, 1993

Bruce "Moose" Ackerson and
David Mokotoff at the wedding
of Penny and Elliott Weinger
December 5, 1993

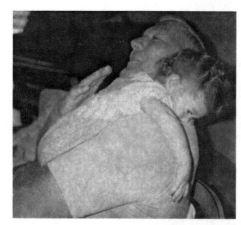

Bruce "Moose" Ackerson with
Emily Mokotoff, 1993

(Left to right):
Tina, Rachel, and Sarah
Mokotoff and Bruce
"Moose" Ackerson at
wedding of Penny and
Elliott Weinger
December 5, 1993

(Left to right):
Meighan and Pam

Dr. Elliott and
Penny Weinger

(Left):
Janey Tribou

Tina Ackerson nursing school
graduation, St. Petersburg,
Florida, 1983

(Left to right): Janey Tribou and Sue Callahan

Meighan Perry

Sean Callahan and cousin Emily
Mokotoff

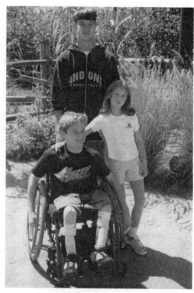

(Clockwise):
Sean Callahan, Emily Mokotoff,
and Brian Callahan

Emily Mokotoff and cousin Brian Callahan

Robert "Bobby" Ackerson

(Clockwise):
Robert "Bobby" Ackerson,
Robert Ackerson "Little Bobby"
and Emily Mokotoff

Robert "Bobby" Ackerson and niece
Brittany Perry, daughter of
Meighan Perry

(Left to right):
Paul "Chip" and wife
Mindy Ackerson,
and Robert "Bobby"
Ackerson

Brittany Perry, Helen Morgan and Emily Mokotoff

Helen and Victor Morgan

(Left to right): Jessie Norton (daughter of Pam Ackerson Barden), Helen Morgan and Tina Mokotoff

Victor Morgan and Emily Mokotoff

Tina Mokotoff, Anna Mokotoff Joseph, (daughter of Eve Mokotoff), Eve Mokotoff, (sister of David Mokotoff), Gertrude and Reuben Mokotoff, (parents of David Mokotoff), Victor Morgan, Sarah Mokotoff, and Helen Morgan

Emily Mokotoff on father's boat "Reel Doc" off St. Pete Beach, Florida

Tina and Emily Mokotoff in Switzerland at final family vacation, 2002

Part Two

The Moose's Children: A Memoir of Betrayal, Death and Survival

"Forgiveness does not change the past, but it does enlarge the future"

–Paul Boese

Tina

---~◦◦~---

David-

I fully understand the reasons you have been about Emily. If the situation were reversed, I would do the same thing. I have been a terrible example and again understand the anger and also the fear Emily feels toward me. I know you are protecting her. You're a good kind man and a wonderful father. My hope is one day we'll be able to both take care of her. 50/50. I do want to be back in her life. I miss her terribly."
Tina, 2003

She could truly light up a room without saying a word. She was young, flirtatious, and her smile beamed boundless rays of light. Her emerald green eyes would twinkle, and her apple cheeks would shine when she laughed. Her full auburn hair, atop her broad shoulders, bounced, as she would walk. Or as she would often tell me how her grandmother described her gait—she didn't walk—she sashayed. I was never sure what that meant, but if you saw her walking, you'd have no trouble understanding it. She was generous to a fault, never missing a chance to give her last dime to a beggar on the street.

But she also had a darker side—the ever-present undercurrent of something terrible that had happened to her as a child, one which would never go away. I never knew much about it until after we were married, and then the chilling and senseless details would pour out of her like a leaky dam. Usually it took sufficient alcohol to fire up the memories, but after a while, she could tell me the same stories sober. At first, I was stunned and unsure about the truth of it all, since she did like to tell stories and embellish reality. However, after her first two stays in alcohol rehab, her sisters provided corroboration. I would listen to her cry about it sometimes, but mostly she just described the abuse in a bland, dry, emotionless fashion, as one would talk about the change in the weather. The matter-of-fact tone would throw me off, and I would jump between polar conclusions such as "this could not have possibly happened," to "she doesn't seem so upset about it now, so she must be over it."

"Vic shoved vodka down my throat when I was eight, and raped me when I was twelve," she would tell me more than once. Mostly, it was in a flat, dissociated tone, which I would come to see often from her and "the sisters." Ironically it reminded me of that joke, "Other than that Mrs. Lincoln, did you enjoy the show?"

And it wasn't just the sexual abuse. "They would beat up my grandmother, and lock her outside the house, whether it was 90 degrees or 30 degrees. We would have to sneak her back in without Vic finding out, or we'd get a beating too."

Or, "When they started drinking, they would start fighting. I remember liquor bottles being smashed on the fireplace and the Christmas tree. When it got really bad, I would hide in my closet, underneath my laundry, cover my ears, and hum as loud as I could so as not to hear them."

"At dinner, we wouldn't have much to eat. We had diluted powdered milk, and mayonnaise sandwiches, while Mom and Vic dined on lobster and steak."

In retrospect, her model for parenting was so skewed, that she showered our daughter, Emily, with gifts, and toys, and adulation, trying perhaps to rewrite the childhood she had lost. It was totally a love of over-compensating, but devoid of what was most important—a steadfast sober parent who a young child could always count on to be there for her, no matter what.

Inherent in the disease of alcohol and addiction, is the inescapable chaos. As Emily and I eventually came to realize, the only thing we could depend upon was that we could not depend upon her. She could be there to take her to dance lessons, or she might be passed out drunk on the floor. She could pick her up on time from school, or not. The abuse and turmoil endured during childhood in the alcoholic home affected all of her siblings as well. Tina was dependable, until she started drinking, and ironically always made fun of her sisters' lack of reliability.

"When is Meighan, or Sue, or Pam coming?" I would ask before a planned visit.

She would wave her hand in the air and say in an amusing fashion, "It doesn't matter when they say they'll be here. I won't believe it until I see the whites of their eyes." Thus, they all came to understand that even their own words and promises were tainted with the stain of childhood distrust and fears of disappointment.

Years later, after Tina had died, I was a few minutes late picking up Emily from school. She called me on my cell phone, hysterical and crying, and afraid that I had forgotten about her. Seeing her disproportionate reaction, we talked about it and she confessed, "It's just that Mom was always late picking me up, and I get scared when that happens still."

"Well, honey," I said. "That was then and this is now. You can count on me." And she always has since.

Tina liked to live large. It wasn't just the alcohol—it was everything. Meal portions were two to three times more than needed, there was never anything like too much sex, and her shopping habits spewed out of control in proportion to her alcohol consumption. With my career at its pinnacle, I certainly had the means to support this addiction, but as her bills started to escalate we would argue and her only defense would be something lame, like, "Oh I don't really spend that much, you should see Lynn at the mall." Or I would ask her to think about returning to work as Emily got older, and got a rebuttal such as, "I have worked continually since I was 12 years-old until Emily was born. I want to be there for her all the time."

My love for her was so great that it blinded me to enforcing commonsense financial decisions such as clothes, cars and vacations. Emily probably traveled with us to more places and countries than I had been to by the time I was 30—Switzerland, Big Sky, Montana, Jackson Hole, Wyoming, Caribbean cruises, Lake Tahoe, California, Park City, Utah, and Beaver Creek, Colorado. The penultimate vacation however was for New Year's Eve, December 31, 1999, for the turn of the century. We went to the Ritz-Carlton resort in Maui for a week of absolute fun and excitement.

Here is what "living large" means. Doing an inventory of her condo after she died, I totaled up the number of clothes in her huge walk-in closet and lost count after 700. Many of them, such as Lucky brand jeans, still had the original sales tags in place. I gave many away to her sisters and took the rest of the decent ones to consignment shops or charities. Her sofas were deep, with over-stuffed matching linen pieces from Ralph Lauren, and a big screen television sat inside of a massive wooden armoire in the living room.

As she crossed that invisible line between drinking heavily and drinking alcoholically, it became embarrassingly impossible to go out with her to social events. At one of Emily's dance recitals, she was blatantly intoxicated, and would hoot, holler, and whistle when Emily danced. And when she wasn't yelling, she would run her hands through one of her friend's hair sitting next to us, cooing how beautiful she was until an offended parent turned around and "shushed" her to be quiet. Later, when she went backstage to get Emily, another dance mom finally dragged Tina out by the hand and snorted to me, "You take her now. I'm tired of babysitting."

She had an uncanny luck for driving while drunk and had neither an accident nor injury to anyone. I took her car keys away from her and forbade her to drive Emily more times than I care to remember. Other than several busted tires, probably from driving over curbs, her Mercedes E-320 station wagon barely had a nick. When Emily had a national dance recital in Las Vegas, she started drinking again on the sly, and then we had a huge public argument while eating dinner with my oldest daughter, Rachel, and her fiancé at the Belliago Hotel, just before a Cirque Du Soleil performance of "O." It got so bad, that I had to get up and leave the table. However, in doing so she grabbed my arm and we began to argue and then got into a tugging match. I don't even remember what the argument was about, but apologized to my daughter, Rachel, and finally got to the show, which I thoroughly hated—stewing in my own thoughts of shame, anger, and embarrassment.

She later succumbed to the alcohol habit of "drinking and dialing." Some of the more memorable calls were explosions like, "I want to talk to my child! Why won't you let me talk to her?" Or, "I'm pregnant! What do you think about that?" Emily and I finally had to block her phone calls. As the list of folks who listened to her complain and chatter dwindled, she even resorted to calling my ex-wife from my first marriage, which I found both comical and appalling. Emily would refuse to go visit her due to her inebriation and public embarrassment, and contact between the two of them faded to nothing. That was November 2003—two months before she died.

Diary entry - March 25, 1992
I don't want to forget the new and important things you have accomplished and will accomplish. I don't know when I'll give you this or how long I'll write, but it is something I want to begin. I'm not the best

with words, but that's not important. What is important is to let you know how much I love you and to give you an idea of our lives together.
    Tina Mokotoff

Tina was never able to personally give Emily the diary from which the passage above was quoted. Emily found it while sorting through her belongings after her funeral, one chilly afternoon in January 2004. She was 12 years old at the time, ironically the same age as when her mother had been raped. To this day, she still has difficulty talking about her mom.

There were so many highs and lows, that it's difficult to know where to begin. When we were dating, I knew she liked to drink more than me, but I rarely saw her drunk, and I had no immediate family experience with alcohol or addiction, other than my father—who was addicted to work.

Paradoxically, Tina's mother and she always seemed close. When I started to hear the tales of her childhood, I couldn't understand the lack of resentment for what had happened. Her own mother failed to protect her, and might even have been tacitly complicit with the abuse by her silence. When queried about this, she and the sisters would always make the same excuse, "Oh it was a bad time. She was always drunk, and didn't know what she was doing."

For the longest time, it seemed that they were content with covering up the incidents, each one dealing with their own demons. It was only after her first stint in rehab did she dare to stir up the old memories and horrors of their past. At family reunions or visits, they would start to drink and talk, comparing notes, about what they remembered. I wasn't present for many of these, but she would always tell me about it after the fact.

While visiting Meighan in Atlanta, Tina came to me late one night in tears.

"What's wrong?" I asked.

"She (Meighan) told me what happened."

"When, where?" I asked dumbfounded.

"You know…when we were little, during one of the bad times."

I nodded.

More sobbing ensued. "She gave herself to Vic as a deal, so he would stop messing with the little ones, (meaning Jodi and Mary)."

I could say nothing but just held her close as she continued to cry until there were no more tears. Her angular jaw and long brunette hair was streaked with the salty wet droplets of her anger and remorse. It seemed if the dam was about to fracture, and the memories were going to pour forth without end, when suddenly the stoical wall went up yet again. I felt lost and overwhelmed. The conversation was over—at least for then.

In the end, it was because of her that the whole knotted ball of twisted and suppressed memories started to unwind. She was the linchpin for the abused children, some of who wanted to talk openly about the abuse, and others who refused. At parties, and family gatherings, where the alcohol was always free flowing, she would start to reminisce with various sisters about their tainted youths. However, it was not until 2002, during an increasingly rare period of her sobriety that she gathered the courage to confront her demons.

We had her mother and stepfather, Helen and Victor Morgan, over for dinner one night. I could tell Tina was fidgety and anxious, but she had given me no clue what she had been planning to say. In hindsight I'm not even certain she had intended it, as the question just seemed to burst out spontaneously.

"Do you remember our house on Greenwood Lane in Lakeland?" she asked both of them. The silence was deafening as Helen's face paled, and Victor looked up from his slurping and threw down his napkin. The implication was obvious to all—that was the house where her rape had occurred.

"We're not going to talk about this," he stammered. "Your mother and I have already thought about leaving the state."

"Why would you do that?" I asked, not believing I could or would say this. "Perhaps there is no statute of limitations in Florida for childhood rape?"

Looking at Helen, who said nothing, he spoke curtly, "This conversation is over. We're leaving." There were no good-byes, or thanks, or apologies. They simply got up and left.

We met rarely with them after that, and any open discussion of her past was quashed as soon as it started. Sinking deeper into depression her drinking accelerated once again, and the intervals of sobriety became shorter and less frequent. I could be nice or mean to her, but it made little difference. If I filed for divorce, she would drink to suppress the anxiety and fear of separation and potential loss of her only child. If we reconciled, (which we did several times) and I withdrew my divorce petition, she would resume drinking in celebration.

Her physical and mental health declined quickly, and as a physician I knew she would not be alive more than one to two years at most. Emily and I were burnt out, and I had little stamina to battle her illness, and so I filed for divorce in September 2003. Tina and I separated in November after an unsuccessful mediation session, to which she showed up late and inebriated. Emily started to refuse visitations with her due to incessant drinking.

"Why are you keeping my daughter from me?" she would scream over the phone to me frantically numerous times.

"I'm not." I would try to explain. "Think about it. It's in my best interest to have her visit you so I can have some free time. However, she won't see you if you're always drunk."

I could've been talking to a door, however as her pickled brain was incapable of processing such simple logic.

"That's bullshit!" She would retort. Then more cursing would ensue and I would have to hang up the phone.

Emily and I spent that New Years' Eve together, and I found her crying in her bed. I tried to comfort her with hugs and rubbed her shoulder, and pleaded with her to talk.

"I don't believe in God anymore," she said between sobs.

"Why not?"

"Because I prayed to him to have mommy stop drinking, and she hasn't."

Thinking for a moment, all I could say was, "You know honey, they say that God helps those who help themselves. Only mommy can stop drinking. God can't do it for her."

I didn't think she was buying it, but at least for the moment, it mollified her and was the best I could come up with to try and explain the unexplainable.

Anyone who has lived with an alcoholic, or an addict, has witnessed the inevitable transformation from a loving and functional person into a self-absorbed conniving narcissist. They become consumed with their fix, or drink, to the exclusion of friends, family, and work. I always thought the term "functional alcoholic" was curious, since even those who continue to work and make a living do so at a reduced and impaired level. For most alcoholics there is that invisible line which gets crossed—the one between drinking heavily, into drinking alcoholically. After the boundary is crossed, the decent into hell is accelerated and rarely do they come back out.

Tina was in rehab twice in 1995, once in 2002, and walked out of another one is 2003. She was Baker Acted three times, (referring to Florida State law BA-52) meaning temporarily held against her will in a hospital, until she was found not to be a threat to herself or others. Usually these episodes preceded a transfer to rehab; however, once I agreed to an early release so she could attend a closing for a condo I had bought her. This was necessary so I could finally extract her from our home.

All the while, her family sat by idly, occasionally wringing their hands, and asking me how she was doing, when they already knew the answer. No one stepped forward to help her—after all how could they? I had excellent medical insurance and the funds to send her to the finest rehab centers. None of it mattered. For in the end, both she and her brother, who could afford none of this high level of care, died within three days of each other. His demise was a drug overdose, supplied by his twin sister's brother-in-law. Hers was alcohol induced gastrointestinal bleeding and aspiration, meaning she choked to death on her own vomit and blood.

Thus, inattention to the core pains planted the seeds for the multi-faceted family dysfunction. Had psychological intervention occurred when she was younger, perhaps the outcome might have been different. In Alcoholics Anonymous they speak about the three "A's." These are awareness, acceptance, and action. In my opinion, she always was stuck in the middle. Never quite able to fully accept that her childhood had been stolen from her, and therefore unable to truly forgive herself and her family. She could never move forward. Only when we can touch a core injury, and it doesn't hurt anymore, is healing possible. For Tina that never happened, and the only way out of the pain became the quick anesthetizing fix of alcohol. Ironically the same thing, which had destroyed her childhood, would end her life.

Helen and Victor

By the time I first met Helen and Victor Morgan in 1987, they were both sober. Tina and I had been dating for a while and we were invited to dinner at their home. Around her stepfather, Tina was always cordial and polite. I saw no indication in her demeanor that would suggest he had brutalized her as a child. Victor had been on the wagon for over thirty years, and Helen, although still enjoying her wine, was rarely drunk, at least when I saw her. They continued to live in the same small house in St. Petersburg, which they had purchased in 1973. Helen worked at Humana, later Columbia-Northside Hospital, as a medical secretary. She was a petite woman whose figure hid well the fact that she had birthed eleven children. She was an excellent cook and a tireless gossiper. When I would make rounds in her unit of the hospital, I would always hear chatter such as, "Oh did you know that Dr. Miller is getting a divorce?" or "Did you hear that Annie Brown just had a miscarriage?"

Victor on the other hand was less affable and just plain odd. Standing about 5'11" he towered over his wife's 5'1" frame. He had a balding head with a few strands of graying comb-over, large glasses, bulbous nose, and eyes that bulged a bit. He reminded me of a taller version of Gollum, the evil half-man half-creature in the Lord of the Rings trilogy. Although less willing to speak and gossip than his wife, he was no less opinionated. His favorite topics were politics, computers, crime, and the police.

Every year at Easter, Helen would make a Sunday brunch, usually consisting of some combination of ham, quiche, turkey, and pasta salads. Approaching the small cinder block home, I was unaware that such hideous crimes and abuse had taken place there decades ago. Tina never confessed to me the truth of her childhood until years after we had married. After that, I was more and more reluctant to even visit their home.

A tall southern oak tree stood sentry near the frail metal carport. Surrounding it was a sparse garden of Mexican petunias, periwinkle, and patches of dying St. Augustine grass. An old window unit air conditioner hung from the front window, dripping rusty water on the walkway and humming a monotonous mechanical tune. Entering the creaking screen door first, and then the painted white wooden door, my nose was struck not by scents of eggs and meat, but rather mold, tobacco, and dog. Vic smoked. Helen had stopped.

Twyla was their scruffy mixed Labrador mutt. Helen had named it after Twyla Tharp, the American dancer and choreographer. It's leathery dark skin showed through black fur in random patches, having been bitten and clawed down by the poor canine that suffered some form of mange. The house had absorbed the dead skin odor of the animal and it seemed deeply embedded in the carpet and furniture, re-circulated by the overtaxed A/C system. After exchanging greetings with the family and assembling a plate, I usually chose to move outside to the backyard to eat.

One warm spring day at their annual Easter brunch, Victor got into a heated argument with his stepson, Bobby. They were discussing the sharing of MP3 music files on-line. Bobby was of medium stature, with a beer belly. He had a simple and somewhat distant affect that made conversing with him difficult. However, one thing was obvious to all around—he and Victor mixed worse than oil and water.

"It's stealing," Victor said.

"No, it's not," said Bobby.

"Someone has paid a copyright for the music and then people like you think they can just lift it for free from the Internet," he retorted.

"If they let it get on the web, then it's in the public domain," Bobby shot back.

"If you're doing it, then you're committing a crime and you should be arrested." Considering his history of child abuse, this seemed ironic.

Voices became louder, fists pounded on the table, and I was certain blows would be exchanged until Helen asserted in a voice louder than usual, "That's enough! Will you two please stop?" Both combatants backed down and the conversation soon changed. As we all stared at the drab grey walls and worn furniture, the air seemed suspended with apprehension. As the old A/C unit groaned, I finally broke the silence.

"How's the job hunting going, Vic?"

In between noisy bites of his ham sandwich due to poor fitting dentures, and loud slurps of his iced tea, he grunted, "Okay," without further elaboration.

Although "retired," both Vic and Helen still needed to work, having squandered most of their money on booze and lavish food and parties in their younger days. Even as Helen's mind began its slow descent into dementia, she continued to work well past the age of sixty-five as a medical secretary, until the hospital let her go, possibly for too many errors. Vic had always bounced from one job to another as a consequence of his drinking. He had worked several times for the *Lakeland Ledger* and the *St. Petersburg Times*, and by the time I met him he was doing some reporting for a small neighborhood newspaper, but quit, or was let go from that as well.

It was only years later when I learned of Bobby's abuse, that I understood the hatred he harbored for Victor. The disdain had nothing to do with sharing of music files—it had to do with childhood rape. He would never talk about it, but, Tina, and most of her sisters, were convinced that Vic had repeatedly sodomized both Bobby and another brother. The anger and tension whenever Bobby and Vic were together was palpable. This was more than just dislike—it was utter contempt and disdain. There were other incidents that pointed to Victor's sexual abuse of his stepchildren. In 1993, when our daughter Emily was about two, Tina and I decided to take a one-week trip to Seattle. At that time I knew very little of Victor's past. I assumed that whatever had happened in the past was a consequence of his alcohol addiction, and since he was now sober, there was no cause for alarm. We let Helen and Vic sleep at our house in Seminole, and after returning home, Tina's sister Meighan was visiting us with her two daughters, Kristin and Brittany. Helen and Vic were still there. Our three daughters played in the pool, while Helen sat outside on a wicker chair, under a Hunter fan, with a glass of wine in hand, and Vic sipped a Coke. Inside the kitchen, I overheard part of a conversation between Tina and Meighan.

"You left Emily with Vic? Are you out of your mind?" Meighan said.

"Mom was here. Nothing happened," Tina responded.

Hearing this now, I couldn't believe that Tina had left Emily with this man. Confronting her later, she admitted perhaps poor judgment, but also assured me nothing had happened. Her belief of course was born of hope, and not any verifiable truth. Emily seemed okay and I willed myself to agree with her conclusion. Both of us were in denial. To this day, I have no evidence that Victor had molested my daughter; however, after that trip we never left Emily alone with him again.

Meighan just shook her head in disbelief as she reached for another glass of white wine. At that time we were living in a custom built house in Seminole, Florida, on a lot embedded with dozens of oak and pine trees. We had a screened-in pool in the backyard. It was August—in Florida—and it was hot. We had only ten neighbors on the small cul-de-sac; Meighan left the house and was chatting with one of them on the street, while Tina and I were preparing to barbeque. I had been marinating a flank steak in my favorite recipe of soy sauce, wine vinegar, sugar, fresh ginger, garlic, scallions, and sesame seeds. I was beginning to prepare my Asian slaw when Kristin, who was six, came running in crying with her bathing suit half pulled down.

"Where's my mommy?" she cried.

Gathering the small child in her arms, Tina asked, "What happened? Are you all right?"

She just continued to wail as her aunt tried to console her. I looked out the family room large bay window and saw Meighan laughing with the neighbor. Exiting through the garage, I waved to get her attention.

"I think you need to come inside," I said to her.

I must have looked concerned, because she didn't ask why or hesitate. Upon entering the kitchen, her distraught daughter ran across the slippery gray tiled floor, almost falling, and launched herself into Meighan's arm. Her curly brown hair still dripping with chlorinated water, she hugged her mother and sobbed. She wouldn't say what happened, but Meighan glanced up and saw Vic in the swimming pool.

Fearing the worse, and like a mother bear protecting her cub, she grabbed Kristin by her shoulders and shook her.

"Tell me what happened!"

Kristin stood dripping and crying in the middle of the kitchen.

"Did he touch you?" Meighan barked again at the little girl.

Terrified, Kristin just stood there is stony silence, fighting back tears. Meighan's protective instincts fired up, and I could see her eyes shoot outside like a laser, focusing on Vic. She did not ask Kristin any more questions, but never left her daughters out of her sight the rest of the afternoon or evening. Just like the bellicose response Vic seemed to elicit from Bobby, the disgust Meighan had for Vic was no less powerful and apparent. She almost never spoke with him, preferring to converse with her mother instead. She, like most of her other siblings, viewed him as a sad and unfortunate attachment to Helen. If there were to be a mother-daughter relationship, his repulsive presence was the price of admission.

Victor Morgan seemed like the perfect foil for Helen. She was outgoing and friendly. He was quiet and subdued, at least when sober. However, when engaged in a conversation, there always seemed to be a simmering cauldron of hatred and hostility. He wasn't just passionate about topics—he defended or attacked them as if his survival hung in the balance of an argument.

In 2002 one of his neighbors was arrested for child pornography. Vic was interviewed on the local television news and gave the usual bland response seen many times.

"He seemed like such a normal guy," he told the reporter.

"No. I had no idea he was involved with that kind of thing."

As I watched his nostrils flare a bit and his brow furrowed, I suspected he was lying. Helen later told me in fact he did know the alleged pornographer and Vic and he had visited often. Helen and Vic were at our house for dinner, shortly after his brief appearance on the evening news. While I was outside cooking hamburgers and fish on the grill, I mentioned I had seen him on television. His response was quick and unequivocal.

"Arresting that guy was a waste of time," he snorted. "The cops should be out arresting real criminals. Watching pornography on a computer is a victimless crime."

I was stunned and could find no words to respond. Not only did he display no sympathy towards the shattered lives of children used for the prurient pleasure of pedophiles, but also his adamant defense of the man convinced me he was aligned in approval with this behavior. If I had ever denied or doubted the truth of his sordid past, in that moment, I knew the real Victor Morgan—a sick, twisted, abuser of innocent children.

After our separation and divorce, I forbade Emily from ever seeing Victor Morgan again. She could see Helen, her grandmother, if *she* wanted to, but it would be without him. Gradually Emily displaced her anger towards Helen and refused to return her letters and phone calls.

The Sisters

There were seven of them, and by age, Tina was somewhere in the middle. She would affectionately refer to all of the others as simply "the sisters." Pam was the oldest and then came Sue. Tina was just a bit older than Janey, (and her twin brother Bobby). The last three she would always call "the little ones." Other than being the youngest, "the little ones" also shared a bond of being raised mostly by their dad, Moose, and his second wife, Jeannie, in Hollywood, Florida. Prior to moving there, they shared another unforgettable distinction: sexual abuse at the hands of Victor Morgan, their stepfather while living with their mom in St. Petersburg. There will be more about this later.

After Tina's third relapse with alcoholism in 2001, she began to talk openly with her sisters about the abuse they had all suffered when they were much younger and living in west central Florida. Most of their memories were repressed until then, and it is likely Tina's brush with death, and her repeated failures at sobriety, rekindled the horrors.

"You can never make peace with yourself until you deal with that part of your life," Pat Shifflet, Tina's psychologist would tell her.

Tina had spoken about this with her therapist on more than one occasion, and in fact, Pat had suggested family therapy. Tina raised this issue with her mother, Helen Morgan, and was met with blunt refusals like, "this is all in the past," or "you imagined a lot of this." It was as if in Helen's mind, it had never happened. Helen was a devout Catholic, and Tina said her mother had "confessed all of her sins to a priest," and therefore felt she was absolved of the whole troubling affair forever.

Undeterred and to her credit, Tina decided her only recourse was to rehash everything with her siblings. Before her death, I pieced together enough of the stories to be convinced that sexual abuse had happened, and to more than one child.

Following Tina's death in 2004, I remained haunted by the stories of her childhood and sought verification from others. After Bruce "Moose" Ackerson died, June 27, 2008 of heart disease, his family decided to scatter his ashes in the Rainbow River behind Sue Callahan's home, (Tina's older sister), in Dunnellon, Florida. Although Moose's son, Bobby had died four years earlier, his twin sister Janey had kept his ashes.

She decided to spread those on the river as well. Dunnellon, a small community situated on the confluence of the Rainbow and Withlacochee Rivers, about ninety miles north of Tampa, is an "old Florida" town. It has an historic train depot and much of its one thousand families are involved in eco-tourism. The rivers are fed by natural limestone springs arising from the Florida aquifer, and are seventy-two degrees all year and crystal clear. "The Bed Restaurant" on North Williams Street, serves eggs, grits, bacon, and pancakes in the morning by waitresses who serve tables in pajamas, and two people can get more food then they can eat for ten dollars.

Sue's small wooden home backs up to the river with old southern oaks, pine, and bald cypress trees. Spanish moss droops everywhere and a worn wooden boathouse sits on the riverbank with a johnboat tied off on the dock. Alligators and egrets lined the heavily weeded shoreline as the family gathered for a ceremony and reunion. It was November, but being Florida it was still steamy.

"You know that Jodi has filed a complaint with the St. Petersburg Police." Sue told me as I sipped a beer and munched on barbeque. Sue could have been Tina's twin in facial features with her perpetual smile and high "apple" cheekbones. However, she was much shorter than Tina and plumper.

"No. I didn't know that," I said.

"Yeah," Sue said. "She's still shaken up over Tina and Bobby's deaths. She and Doug (her husband) are separating and she's having a hard time with all of the bad memories."

I didn't have to ask Sue to be more specific—I already knew.

A few minutes later, I saw Jodi down near the water and decided to ask her about it. Doug was there but as he broke away from Jodi I approached her. I gave her a big hug and kiss on the cheek.

"Your kids look so grown up now—do you have four or five?" I asked, fumbling for a neutral question.

"Five," she said, and named them off, pointing each one out as they ran on the sloped grassy lawn chasing Sue's Golden Retriever, Spice.

Jodi was thin, medium height with hair that alternated between brown and blond, depending upon her mood. She smiled less than Sue, but like all of Tina's sisters, had always been open and kind with me.

"How's Emily doing?" She asked. "Is she here?"

"She's great. Yes, she's up there with Lexi and Summer," I said pointing to Jodi's two oldest daughters on the porch.

"She's gorgeous and so grown-up," Jodi exclaimed.

After a pause I said, "Sue told me you had filed a complaint with the police, is that true?"

"Yes," she said in a subdued voice. I could see her head bend forward a bit as she frowned, shoulders slumped.

"I think that was very brave of you," I said.

"I don't know if anything will happen with it, but I can't look at Vic anymore without getting sick—especially after Tina and Bobby died. It's just been eating away at me—like a cancer. Look at him there," she said in disgust, pointing a finger towards Vic who was standing close to Helen near a hammock, slurping his food.

"Does he know yet?" I asked.

"No, but he will soon enough. Right now the police detectives are interviewing some of the other sisters, and after that they will most likely question him. I hope he goes to jail forever," she said, and with that she spat at the grass, hands and body trembling.

"I'm thinking about writing a book about Tina's life. Do you think I could interview you some time about your childhood? I know it might be painful, but your input would be an enormous help," I said.

"If it would help put that bastard away, then I'm all for it," she answered.

"I don't know about that, but it might help me with some closure," I said.

Jodi shifted a bit and watched as Doug started to come back towards us, and she said, "I will call you next month. We'll be in St. Pete again to meet with the detective."

"Thanks," I said, turning my head towards Doug and shaking his hand. As I started to walk away, he said to his wife, "What was that all about?"

"Nothing important. We were just catching up on old times," she said avoiding the issue.

Doug would later be told of everything that had occurred and was supportive of Jodi's actions, even driving with her from South Florida to St. Pete and meeting with the States Attorney's office.

In that moment, I felt compelled to interview as many of the family members as I could in order to reconstruct the nightmares of their childhood. At age seventy-eight, and in poor health, I was under no illusion that Vic's crimes from decades ago would result in incarceration. However, I was now committed to try. In person interviews seemed the best way to reconstruct those lost years. Upon contacting all of the sisters, they agreed. Pam, Tina's oldest sister, contacted another brother and this is what she said, "I spoke to X. and he doesn't want his name mentioned in the book. He wants no part of it. He said he's wiped that out of his life, never to be thought of again." Thus in all subsequent sibling dialogue, I have named him only as "X."

I approached each interview with some trepidation, knowing full well that I would be uncovering deeply held secrets and reticent memories that most of them would otherwise choose to forget. Yet, I needed to separate the fact from fiction. Moreover, without their help as witnesses, Victor Morgan would stay forever invisible. I did not want to let that happen again.

What follows are a series of interviews I conducted with "the sisters" during 2009 and 2010. Although the memories of their childhood between 1968-1974 vary somewhat, there is more corroboration than there is disparity. All of the sisters were certain that Victor had sodomized Bobby, and one other brother who adamantly declined to be interviewed. Bobby died of a drug overdose on January 5, 2004. In October 2010, I was able to interview his ex-wife in Lakeland, Florida. For the most part, the surviving women were open and honest about their past, and as difficult as it was to talk about, I do not believe any thing described was imagined or manufactured. I also wanted to give them validation of the crimes that time and the justice system had taken away.

Janey

She had always been one of Tina's favorite sisters. Yet even after we were married, she remained an enigma to me. Aloof and quite private, Tina had scoffed that she had escaped the hell of their childhood by running off as a teenager to marry the "bug man." Her husband, Richard (Dickie) Tribou, was indeed in the pest control business, and he often shunned family gatherings. Gruff and demanding, Tina said he had tobacco, marijuana, sex and beer addictions. He would leer at my daughters and make lewd comments about teenage girls—even relatives. Oafish comments like, "My Kelly you are looking fine!" were not unusual. Age had not been kind to him—he had a beer belly, thinning hair, and gray-black goatee beard. Tina would say they had a great marriage, but later imply they were on the precipice of divorce. Their kids seemed honest and hard working, and if Janey had any addictions, she hid them well. She appeared to be a great mother, wife, and co-breadwinner. Months following my encounter with Jodi at the "spreading of ashes" ceremony, I called her and she agreed to meet me for lunch. Since we both lived in the same city, she was quite accessible, and therefore an ideal sister to meet with first. She chose the Red Mesa, a southwestern restaurant, on Fourth Street in St. Pete, because it was close to her work at a day care center, and the food was good. It was a cool crisp January day, and we hugged inside the front door. Dressed in simple dark winter tones she carried herself tall and self-assured except for one flaw—her teeth were crooked and some were broken. Tina had said she and Dick had no health or dental insurance—perhaps that is why she only half-smiled, self-conscious of poor dentition. The hostess seated us without delay. The waitress took our drink order—two iced teas, and asked, "Are you ready to order yet?"

I looked at Janey, and she seemed to be familiar with the menu.

"I'll have the Southwest BBQ shrimp, please," she said not even looking at the menu.

"Do you mind if I record this?" I asked.

She smiled. "No, of course not."

I pushed the record button, and laid it flat on the table.

"Tell me what you first remember about your mom and dad?" I asked.

"I don't even remember my mother. But I have so many vivid memories of my dad." She sat up in her chair, back quite straight, expressionless, her face without either a smile or frown—green eyes just fixed upon me. Her tall thin figure hid well the usual middle-aged female bodily aftereffects of four pregnancies.

"What kind of memories?" I probed.

"So many. Like when we lived out at the beach, he would come into our bedroom at night waving a dead squirrel and trying to scare us. I remember sitting in the bathroom watching him shave."

"Do you remember when your mom and dad divorced?"

"No. I was only five and I don't remember that at all."

"What was your first memory of Vic?'

"We moved from St. Pete to Lakeland—to another big house. Vic worked as a reporter for *The Lakeland Ledger*, (the local newspaper). But that was a real bad time. I must have been seven or eight. We had a pull out couch and I think it was Tina and I sleeping in it. I remember him coming in one night and lying down in between us. I remember thinking that this was odd, and even at a young age, I was very uncomfortable. Then he reached his hand between my legs and molested me."

"Did you scream or resist?"

"I just pushed him away and then he left."

"Did you ever tell your mom or any of your sisters?"

"No," her head briefly turned down and for a moment, we lost eye contact. I decided to leave it alone for now.

"What else do you remember?"

"We were locked outside of the house a lot, even on hot summer days. Then one night we got back into the house, and I remember that they were drunk as hell, and fighting, and I remember being hit with a belt buckle."

"Why did he hit you?"

"I don't remember."

Shifting the subject a bit, I asked, "So when did you move back to St. Pete from Lakeland?"

Her face remained calm, and as she spoke, her voice was neither animated nor dramatic, just monotone, as she might be reading a news report. She cracked a small smile; again revealing some needed dental work that she could not afford.

"A few years later—I was maybe eleven or twelve—that was a bad time too. We had a friend, Alan Furtado, do you know him?"

"Yes."

"One day he took us ice skating at the mall, and I fell, and someone slashed me with a skate. I still have the scar on my leg. Well, my mom didn't take me to the doctors for three days, and by the time I got to the doctor my leg was so infected."

"Your meals will be here shortly," said the waitress, oblivious to our conversation. She quickly plunked down the iced teas.

Both of us nodded as she scurried off to the next table.

I nodded. "What else?"

"Mom and Vic fought a lot. I remember seeing marks and bruises on her. One day my mom and I were sitting on the porch and he came out with a shotgun, and hit her in the side of the head with it."

"Do you remember why?" I asked

She shook her head no as she sipped her tea.

"Did he ever molest you again?"

She paused for a moment before speaking.

"We had bunk beds. I was in the top one and I don't remember who was in the bottom. But he came up to mine and laid next to me. But I just turned away. By this time I was old enough to know what was going on, you see. But again I never said anything to anyone."

"That's very common," I said.

"Is it really?" she asked seeking assurance.

"Yes."

"And I really never knew what happened to everyone else until after Tina and you were married."

"Really?" I responded.

"Yup."

The waitress appeared again, placing the plates of hot BBQ shrimp and rice in front of us.

"Can I get you anything else now?" she asked.

"No thanks," I answered before Janey even had a chance.

"I'll check back with you in a little while then," she said. I had hopes she wouldn't—she was breaking up my rhythm and train of thought.

"How about your Dad? Where was he when all of this was happening?"

"He had moved to Hollywood, (Florida), and had married Jeannie. He would come to St. Pete occasionally but never to our house. He would just pick me up from work and we'd go out and he'd buy me something. I loved my Dad, but he wasn't really a very good dad."

"How's that?"

"Well, he would buy us stuff, but he'd never talked to us about Mom or Vic. I really don't think he knew." *(Or perhaps didn't want to know, I thought.)*

"My Dad came up one day and took X., I remember that. Then he came up and got Meighan, Mary and Jodi as well." (Her three younger sisters.)

"So all of the younger ones?"

"Yes."

We ate our shrimp and I thought about my next question, but she dropped her fork and looked at my eyes without hesitation.

"All I can say is Vic destroyed a family. He got everyone of us, including Bobby and X."

"You mean raped or molested...even the boys?"

"Um-um."

"I think the reason Tina and Bobby are dead are because of him. Bobby, (Janey's twin brother,) told me so many times 'I wish I were dead,' and I blame that on Vic. He, (Bobby) used so many drugs and drank so much until well; you know it just killed him. He destroyed your family and my family and all of our families. One night after you guys were divorced, I remember Kelly (her daughter) and I spending the night at Tina's condo. On the phone Tina sounded fine, but by the time we got over there she was so drunk—she reminded me of my mom. Then she told me how Vic had raped her, and I really didn't know until that night."

"I understand that you and Jodi finally went to the police here?"

"Yeah. I just did that for Jodi. But unless someone else will testify they won't prosecute him, and no one else will talk about it, and of course Tina and Bobby are dead. However, the police are still investigating, so maybe something will happen eventually."

"When did you move out from home?" I asked.

"When I was seventeen, I just had to get out. I knew my Dad would be upset if I just moved in with Dick, (her husband), so we just got married."

"Are you all finished?" The waitress asked. "Any coffee or dessert?"

We shook our heads; I paid the bill, and after a polite hug, I thanked her for taking the time to talk to me. She thanked me for lunch, then quickly put on her scarf and brown leather jacket. I watched her and again marveled at her slim figure. As we walked out the door of the restaurant to our separate cars, her rhythmic stride reminded me of Tina's sway. It was a cold winter day in St. Petersburg—around 55 degrees, fall or spring weather if you lived up north of course. She had always been one of Tina's "cool" sisters. By cool, I don't mean seventies-style neat or hip, but so calm on the outside and never dramatic. From our conversation, I still couldn't figure out how she remained so devoid of apparent emotion, but concluded that her detached manner was perhaps a way of dealing with the pain. She had become emotionally numb. Driving away in the dry and windy January air, I tried to forget once again the things I had tried to forget so many times before.

Mary

Sitting down on the soft brown over-stuffed couch, I could smell the still present odor of Lydia, her large, but gentle German Shepard. Over her shoulder, a miniature wall grandfather clock's pendulum swung slowly back and forth. It chimed on the hour and half hour, but not at all in sequence with several other large antique wood floor clocks. Speaking with little outward emotion, her blond highlighted hair caught the mid-afternoon sun's rays, accenting her angular face and jaw. I took a swallow of my beer, and started asking questions.

"So, when I talked to Janey, she said she didn't remember your mom much, only your dad. Was it the same for you?"

Mary, nicknamed Penny by her family, did not hesitate in her answer. "I remember living in Villa Grande." (The street where the large marital home had been located in St. Pete.) "I was only three when they got divorced, so I don't remember anything about them together. All I remember about living at Villa Grande was the pool area. Then we moved to Lakeland and I don't remember much about that either. Then we moved to the place in Shore Acres (a St. Pete neighborhood). Is that right?" I was surprised by her question—assuming I would know fine details of *her* childhood.

"Yes, I think so," I said, recalling the time-line described by Janey.

"And that's when everything started for me—at least in my memory."

"What is it that you remember?"

We sat in silence for a few seconds as I listened to the metronome sound of the clocks. She shifted her slender torso slightly and looked uncomfortable—not from the couch—but with body language that telegraphed she would like to be somewhere else, like shopping—anything but having to relive this all over again. We made eye contact but her gaze was through or past me. I was reminded of the empty stares on newly freed Holocaust concentration camp victims, seen so often on black and white photographs. It was an empty and numb gaze.

"We use to swim off of the dock, and Jodi almost drowned because she didn't have her bubble on. Then one Christmas, Grandma bought Vic some cologne bottles and he threw every single one against the wall. I remember not being able to sleep at night because I would hear footsteps and it would be Vic in the garage. He would lock Grandma in there and throw away her glasses, and then she couldn't see. And...uh...back-up. I do remember back in Lakeland, and this is really disgusting, and I really can't stand saying this. But I do remember a few birthday parties, where my Mom and Vic would run around without any clothes on. Then he would make us sit on his lap."

She paused, as if waiting me for me to prompt her.

"So he would put you on his lap, and he was naked." I said. "Then what?"

"I really don't remember what happened after that."

I decided to let it go for now.

"Then back at Shores Acres, after I had my tonsils out, I remember Vic picking me up, swinging me around, and then dumping me in a metal garbage can, and I cut my foot on a piece of glass. And on one Fourth of July he made me shoot a sawed-off shotgun and I had a big bruise on my shoulder."

She kept fencing me off with lots of, "I don't remember, really. I guess I just blocked everything out." Over and over again, almost like a mantra, it was, "I really don't remember."

"What then?" I asked

"From Shore Acres, we moved to the Playtime Motel."

"I didn't know about that. How many of you were there?" I asked.

"Well Tina was going out with Billy a lot and Janey was with some Fred guy, so it would be me, Jodi, Meighan, X., Bobby, Vic, Mom, and Grandma."

"In one room?"

"No. Two."

"How long did you all live in the motel?"

"It seemed like a long time, but it might have been only one or two weeks. I don't recall, but it was disgusting and gross, and they were drunk all the time then. Then we moved into the house where they live now in St. Pete. And that is you know the real disgusting part. All five girls were in one bedroom. Bobby and X. were on the pullout couch in the living room. Grandma was in one bedroom and Mom and Vic were in the third one. And every day they were drunk, and then the police would come a lot."

"Why?"

"I don't remember."

"I do remember telling Tina and Janey what Vic was doing to me and Jodi. But nothing was ever done about it." She said.

"So what happened? Just tell me your personal experience if you could."

The clock chimed over her head again.

"I uh, well, I mean, he would touch me and make me tickle his back. But nothing major, like I heard from my other sisters. Then he would violate me."

"What do you mean exactly?" I pressed.

"He would place a finger inside my vagina."

I nodded. "But you weren't raped?"

"No, not that I can remember." It seemed unlikely she would forget something as painful as a rape.

She continued. "He would beat Grandma up all the time and he was unmerciful."

"So you all talked about it then, but I guess it really came out many years later. Is that correct?"

"Yeah. It was after you and Tina were married and she started to talk about it a lot. Tina and Janey were the only ones I ever told, not any of the other kids. But I kind of think that Bud and Chip, (two of her older brothers), probably knew."

"How's that?"

"By the way they treated Vic. They were always ready to fight and probably could have killed him. I just remember the drunkenness in my life and how bad it was. Jodi and I would pour out their vodka bottles and fill them with water. I never got caught, but I knew they might kill me if they found out. Then the police would come and always ask us 'Are you okay?' and of course we'd always say yes, because I didn't want to go stay at some stranger's house." (Meaning a foster home.)

She didn't fidget or move on the couch and her face was an unemotional mask of stoicism. Once or twice, I could hear her voice start to crack or waver, but she would always recover to a place of strained emotional control.

"So how did you finally come to move down to Hollywood?" I asked.

"One day, when I was twelve, and Mom and Vic were drunker and

137

meaner than usual, Jodi and I just left the house and walked down to the 7-11, because we didn't even have a phone at the house. I called my Dad from the payphone, and I told him to come and get me. He said okay, and I told Jodi to pack her stuff and told her he was coming to get us the next day."

"Just you two?" I asked.

"Yes. X. had already gone down to live with him a few months before. We didn't tell Mom until my Dad came, and when I finally told my Mom I was in a panic. She wasn't very happy and she screamed and yelled. But Jodi and I took all of our stuff in pillowcases and we just left."

"Was Vic there when you two left?" I asked.

"No. I don't know where he was, maybe drunk on his ass in his room."

"Was he working?"

"Hell no," she scoffed. "He was too drunk to work. I don't know how my Mom kept her job at the hospital, as much as she drank. The only time she stopped drinking was when I would pretend I was sick and she had to take me to the doctor. Then she would tell me to go back to school and she would start drinking again."

"When did Meighan come down?"

"Much later and it was weird, but after being with my Dad for a while, I wanted to move back. Can you believe that—as horrible as it was? But there's always that bond with your Mom, you know?"

I don't know that I agreed with her, and wondered to myself if this wasn't more a manifestation of "The Stockholm Syndrome." The syndrome describes the behavior of kidnap victims who, over time, become sympathetic to their captors. The name derives from a 1973 hostage incident in Stockholm, Sweden. At the end of six days of captivity in a bank, several kidnap victims actually resisted rescue attempts, and afterwards refused to testify against their captors. Captives begin to identify with their captors initially as a defensive mechanism, out of fear of violence. Small acts of kindness by the captor are magnified, since finding perspective in a hostage situation is by definition impossible. Rescue attempts are also seen as a threat; since it's likely the captive would be injured during such attempts.

It's important to note that these symptoms occur under tremendous emotional and often physical duress. The behavior is considered a common survival strategy for victims of interpersonal abuse, and has been observed in battered spouses, abused children, prisoners of war, and concentration camp survivors.

Her face finally became more animated and the pitch in her voice rose a bit. "Yes," I said.

"But my Dad wouldn't let me, and thank God I didn't."

Mary had been in alcohol rehab twice, but has managed to stay sober for the past five years, married to her first and only husband, a Hollywood orthopedic surgeon, Elliot Weinger. Mary had been his office assistant, and they had an affair. Later he would divorce his wife. The latter was a long messy ordeal, which ultimately ended with his estranged wife moving to Los Angeles with their three children. The doctor and his ex-wife continue to battle about money in court to this day. Elliott had always been taken with the finer things in life—big house, boat, antiques, ski trips to Vail, Colorado, and a Porsche. Tina and I had attended their wedding at the stylish Turnberry Resort in Miami, and I recall one of the snippy female guests gossiping with a friend, saying, "Can you believe this—and she can't even cook."

As with her sister, Tina, it didn't take Mary long to start idolizing the finer things in life, spending more time in the finer stores of Aventura Mall. Today, she stays busy working in Elliott's office, shuttling their son, Zach, around to hockey games, and trying very hard not to remember.

Jodi

~~~∿ჟ७∿~~~

All buildings have to start from something. After the site is dug and prepared, and footers sunk into the ground, then a block, or brick, needs to be placed in order to support the rest of the structure. Once the foundation is created, and it is judged to be strong, only then can the rest of the structure begin to take shape and be created. One sister needed to come forward, needed to take action, and start the process of unraveling what had happened to them as children. Without that one assertive person, the only thing left would be idle gossip, rumor, and innuendo, leading to nowhere. That one person was Jodi.

In the winter of 2009, she drove from South Florida to St. Petersburg, along with her husband Doug, to face a St. Petersburg Police Department detective's questions about what had happened to her years ago. My present wife, Denise and I, offered our house for her and Doug to stay over. They declined, preferring to stay at a motel, but agreed to come over for dinner. With five beautiful children, whom they left back home with family, we sat around the dinner table eating home made pizzas, salad, and beer. As an Ackerson girl, who rarely passed up a beer or glass of wine, I was surprised when she asked for water only. We talked about our families and children, and after dinner was cleaned up, I asked to speak with her privately in my study.

She sat on my futon, looking uncomfortable, but more than willing to speak freely. She would tell me everything that she would tell the St. Petersburg Police Department detective the following morning. Her long brown hair, streaked with blond highlights, lay upon her high cheekbones, a physical trait she had inherited from her father. For just a moment, I thought I was seeing Tina again, possessing those same rounded facial features that had been such a prominent part of Moose's face. Jodi has always been thin, however, after five children, some middle-age padding had started to accumulate in her thighs and tummy. But she still looked quite fit and attractive. She leaned forward on the edge of the pillow seat, her hands folded on her lap, her expression serious.

"Can you take me back to your first memory of your Mom and

Dad?" I started.

"My mom was ironing and watching soaps, and I didn't want to take a nap. But she made me anyway."

"St. Pete or Lakeland?"

"Lakeland."

"What was your first memory of Vic?"

"We were at Playtime Motel and I don't think I had bathed in days and I wanted to bathe so bad. And my mom made liver, and I didn't want to eat liver. Somehow or other I was made to sit on liver. Then I told one of my sisters that I was so itchy, I just needed a bath. Then one of them, I think maybe it was Tina or Janey, finally got me a bath—but we had to sneak it. Then I got an infection on my leg, and my grandma had to take care of it. That was my first memory of him."

"So he was the one who made you sit on the liver?"

"Yeah. After I wouldn't eat it."

"What's the next thing you remember about him?"

"From the motel we moved to Shore Acres. I remember being on a boat and only being allowed to wear my bottoms, and not my top."

"How old were you?"

"I'm not sure…maybe five or six."

I watched her, motionless, fingers intertwined on her lap. Her voice didn't waiver nor did she hesitate to answer. I saw the same matter-of-fact, but sad look I had seen with Janey and Mary.

Jodi had moved to Hollywood, Florida along with Mary, Meighan, and X. in the late 1970's. She later married Doug Lane, a construction worker, and they subsequently had five children, Alexis, Summer, Clay, Jade, and Cal. She opened a day care center and when hard economic times fell upon the Florida economy the construction industry came to a virtual standstill, so Doug helped out there as a handyman. They have been separated more than once, and at this writing are finally divorced.

"I remember Vic kicking me out of a boat and I almost drowned. Someone saved me, but I don't remember who it was. I remember there being lots of parties, but what I recall the most was when we moved to St. Pete. That's when all of the horrible things started. My Grandma was a savior, and Pam and Janey saved me, but I have pretty much only bad memories."

"How did they save you?"

"My Grandma saved me from Vic numerous times. He and my mom were drunk 24/7. I went to Pam's house every summer. (Her oldest sister who was living in Plant City at the time.) And Janey would come and get us out of the house like at two in the morning, and Tina would always take me if she went out on a date, just to get me out of the house."

"Can you tell me what they saved you from?"

"From everything, really," her voice started to quicken and shake. "Since they were always drunk, they never fed or bathed us. They would have steak for dinner while we ate only bread. They were physically and verbally abusive, and poor Grandma was there alone, but she would never leave my mom. They would just drink non-stop, from the moment they awoke until they passed out at night, and me and Mary and Meighan would just dump out their vodka bottles."

"How long were you there?"

"Six years. I left when I was twelve. My Dad tried to get us out of there, but every time he would come, she would stop drinking and she would tell us she would teach us how to sew and cook, you know so she looked like the perfect mother, and she would do that for about a week. And of course, you know you love your mom, and so you don't want to leave. I loved my mom then."

"And now?"

She didn't hesitate. "Now I can't stand her. I don't have any relationship with her."

"How did you finally leave then?"

"Finally my dad just came and got us without my mom knowing. My Grandma knew though."

"Did you all leave together?"

"No. X. left first, then Mary, then me, and finally Meighan."

"Where were your older sisters and brothers?"

"They all just left, because they uh, thought we would be okay with Grandma."

Having already spoken to Pam and Sue, I knew this wasn't true. Both had expressed a lot of guilt and remorse at abandoning the younger siblings. I chose not to pursue it.

"Can you tell me about the bad stuff?"

She bit her lip and paused.

"They would have sex under the big tree in the front yard, and the police would come, but they never caught them. Mom would go to work, God only knows how, and then she would leave us with only Grandma and Vic. He was mean and hateful. He would beat me with a rope. He would threaten to kill Grandma and throw us all outside at two in the morning. He'd wake us up and kick us out of the house."

"Did you see any of your brothers or sisters molested?"

"No. Just me."

"What happened?"

"He would ask me to come into his room and scratch his back, and then he'd make me touch him, while he was naked, on his penis." She picked up her right hand, stared at it and said, "If I could cut off this hand I would. Then he would touch himself and make me touch myself and then he would touch me. But I don't remember any penetration."

"Would he masturbate?"

"No. He made me do that for him."

"Do you think your Dad had any idea about this?"

"No. He knew about the drinking, but when he finally found out about Tina—after she died—he was devastated. Once Tina started to talk about it, everyone started to speak out as well. Meighan told me she walked in once and saw Vic on top of Tina."

"Did you ever tell your mom?"

"Yes, but not until after Tina died. I decided to confront her because I now knew Tina was fed alcohol when she was eight, and raped by Vic, and this was big for me because I had never told a soul—why I don't know. So anyway I called my mom and told her that Tina wasn't lying, and then she said that Tina had told Vic the day before she died that she was sorry for lying about him. I was shocked, so I asked Tina later that day, before she died, if she said that to Mom, and Tina said no. So if she wants to believe the lies from a man who has raped or molested most of her children, well then that's her problem, but I'm not buying it. So then I told her what had happened to me and you know what she said?"

"No, what?"

"She said, 'Well Jodi, I know that you believe that is what happened to you because your Grandmother put that it your head.' My grandmother never put that in my head, and I knew she was lying too because my grandmother never knew. Again, I never told a soul until well after Tina died. Mom asked me if I still loved her, and I told her she was my mother, but I would never speak to her again in my life. I was so upset that I called Pam after I got off the phone and she called Mom. Mom called me right back and asked me what it was I wanted her to do. She even asked me, 'So you want me to call the police?' and I said 'No mom, I want you to acknowledge that your son and daughter didn't die in vain, and that I'm not lying to you, and there are many others."

"What did she say to that?" I asked.

She said, "I believe you."

"That's it?"

"No. There's more. After my dad died last year, Kristin, (Meighan's daughter), and I had a conversation. She told me she had a dream, and you have to remember that Kristin never knew what had happened to me, and described exactly the same thing that had happened between me and Vic when I was a child."

"Hold on a minute," I interrupted her. "Are you saying that Vic may have molested the grandkids as well?"

"Yes, and I said, 'Kristin honey, I'm not sure that it was a dream.' Then I called her mom, and unfortunately Meighan was drunk at the time and said she was going to call our mom. I pleaded with her not to do that, but she did anyway. Then my mom called me to argue and I asked her to put Vic on the phone. At first she said no, but finally she did. I told him he had two choices here, you can tell the truth and at least acknowledge what you did to me, or I can go to the police."

"You're a liar," is all he said to me.

"Anything else?"

"Nope."

"So Janey and I went to police department, filed the complaint, and that's why I have to come back and speak with them tomorrow."

I could see that she was spent, but determined to see this through to some conclusion. Her shoulders slumped forward a bit, as if a weight had been removed, and we both rose, and hugged.

"I'm proud of you," I said. "This took a lot of courage."

She nodded her head, and we walked downstairs, where Doug was waiting for her. I shook his hand, and walked them both to the front door. All of us knew that once this line had been crossed, there was no turning back.

"You can give the detective my cell phone number if he needs corroboration of Tina's story."

"Thanks," she answered.

"Oh Jodi, by the way, I think you are doing the right thing here. I don't think any of you can truly start to heal until this all comes out in the light of day. No more secrets or lies."

She nodded her head and as they drove off into the cool humid night, it struck me that I too couldn't heal completely either until this was finally over. Five years after Tina's death, and I was still deluding myself that I had come to peace with everything that had happened. Perhaps her honesty and bravery would open the avenue to finding some peace myself.

Meighan

I was down to my last witness. Bobby and Tina were dead, and three of the other sisters had been open and honest about having been fondled by Vic. Jodi was clear that he had subjected her to mutual masturbation. Meighan had reportedly seen Tina's rape. She and I had some history together, so I assumed she would be upfront and candid with me. Her second husband, David Jenks, had recently divorced her because she couldn't stop drinking, and she too had been to rehab. However, she was in Atlanta, and rumored to have been drinking again, and all signs certainly pointed that way to me. No return phone calls, text messages, or emails. No one knew her address. As an experienced neonatal ICU nurse, and still working, she had to be sober some of the time—or at least I hoped. I told her a month in advance when I would be in town, and she promised we would get together. However, as the time approached, she somehow found herself working the three days I would be there. Getting her to commit to a time and location to meet was like trying to nail Jell-O to a wall. Not to be turned down, I finally got her to consent to a morning break while working a 12-hour shift.

Growing up she was elfin, and had a face so round, that her family had nicknamed her "Muffin." The name stuck until well after her first divorce and her move from Hollywood to St. Pete. In an act of independence, she finally declared her name was Meighan, and told her family not to call her Muffin any more. I remember her as the jokester in the family. Petite and lively, she was always visiting Tina and I with her two daughters, while she worked at All Children's Hospital in St. Pete. She even dated my best friend, Steve Greenberg. Twenty years her senior, post-divorce, and in no mood to ever marry again, he repeatedly dismissed her marital proposals, until finally one day she gave him the dreaded female ultimatum of "We either do this, or I walk." He once again refused her offer and she chose the latter.

She walked into the arms of a hospital heart catheter sales rep, David Jenks, and they were married six weeks later on her rebound. His company relocated to Atlanta, and it didn't take long for him to realize he had a tiger by the tail. Free spirited on the outside, she was as much tortured inside as Tina and Bobby. It wasn't long before she and her overly controlling husband began to bicker. They had a baby— she claimed by accident—and then the demons rose again with the stress of the marriage, work, and a newborn. Alcohol was, as usual, both the problem and the solution. Her sober days lessened, and her husband grew increasingly less patient. He threatened her with a simple choice—divorce or rehab. She chose the latter.

Sobriety didn't last long, and ultimately not only did she lose him, but she lost custody of her daughter too. How she kept working and drinking, I will never know—actually I didn't want to know. I had not seen her in years. Maybe every other year she would call me to chat about Steve and old times. One year it was New Years' morning when my cell phone went off and she went on and on, reminiscing about the past.

"We really need to get together you know," she would babble. " You should see Kristin and Brittany (her daughters) now. They are so grown up and beautiful."

"I know," I said. "Emily keeps up with them on Facebook." I didn't hear from her again for two years.

Then came the family reunion and ash-spreading ceremony in Dunnellon, Florida in November 2008. Emily and I went, and I started to hear the details of Jodi's complaint filed with the St. Petersburg Police Department. Meighan and her daughters were at the reunion.

I almost did not recognize Meighan. She had always been small, about 4'11' and barely 100 pounds. She was now overweight and blown up like a Macy's Day balloon float. Her face and eyes were swollen, as were her legs and belly. I assumed liver failure, and déjà vu struck me. I couldn't bring myself to fib and say, "You look good."—I'm not that good of a liar. So I settled instead for, "It's nice to see you again." She was obviously drunk.

"Aren't my girls beautiful?" she gushed rhetorically, tipping to one side. "And look at Emily…she's gorgeous!" Then grabbing her cell phone, she started to dial, saying, "Let's call Steve!"

I shook my head. "I don't think that would be a good idea really."

Fortunately she hung up the phone, and we talked about a variety of unimportant and mundane subjects. Five minutes later, I excused myself to visit with others.

Time had not been kind to her. Five months later, in Atlanta, she looked just as bad, maybe even worse. The swelling around her eyes had grown, she still looked six months pregnant, and her arms and ankles bulged with fluid stretching the green cotton material of her size small scrub uniform. I sat with my coffee cup in a comfortable over-stuffed chair near the gift shop on the first floor of Northside Hospital, where she worked. Overcast light streamed through the second story atrium skylights onto the large potted green tropical plants, which matched her scrubs. I didn't have much time, and thought a second chance at an interview with her would be dicey. She told me her break was for only fifteen minutes, so I came right to the point. I turned the tape recorder on.

"Tina told me that she had been raped by Vic when she was twelve."

"Um-hum," she nodded in agreement.

"I guess it happened in Lakeland."

"Um-hum."

"One of the girls said that you had walked in and saw this…"

"Um-hum," she kept saying repeatedly.

"Right," she now added.

"So is that true?"

"Um-hum."

"Did it happen more than once?"

"I only saw it one time," she answered, wanting this inquisition to be over without delay. She had that look of, "Why did I ever agree to do this?" and appeared uncomfortable, despite showing a brave mask. I knew Meighan well enough to know that she was stone cold sober, and telling the truth, as she shot back hurried answers without even thinking or hesitating.

"And my understanding from speaking with you before is that you too were raped or molested by him as well?"

Not missing a beat, she quickly corrected me, "Not raped, but molested."

"And you cut some kind of deal with Vic to protect Mary and Jodi?"

"Right."

"Well, the state's attorney said last week she wants to talk to you…"

"She'll do it on the phone right?" she asked cutting me off.

"Yes. That's my understanding," and she nodded her head.

"Getting back to living with your Mom and Vic—you were the last child to leave, right, and go down to Hollywood to live with your Dad?"

"Yes."

"Do you remember how long you lived in Lakeland?"

"No. I have hardly any recollection, except for the bad stuff."

"Bad stuff in St. Pete and Lakeland?"

"Oh yeah, especially in Lakeland, because that's when I walked in on him. He was on Tina—on the pull-out couch."

I had to be careful with my words here. "On" seemed to be important, and could be interpreted several ways.

I played my tape back later and what she had said exactly was, "…that's when I walked in ON him…ON Tina—on the pull-out couch."

"Did you say anything to your Mom at the time?"

"Uh-uh, no, I don't remember." I had some doubts about the veracity of that answer.

"Pam said that maybe Vic had stumbled into the wrong room."

She interrupted again, "Except it wasn't in a room. It was in the living room. Like I said, on the pull-out couch."

"What happened after that?"

"I remember Bud and Chip (her older brothers) beating Vic up." This matched Pam's story as well.

I pressed on. "What about X.? Everybody says that they think he was abused like Bobby, but no one seems really sure."

"I am sure that things happened between Vic and X. He's afraid that if he opens it up it will affect him in a bad way."

"I get that, but I feel like you have to go through it someway someday."

"Um-hum."

"How about your kids? Are they good?"

"Oh yeah," she answered.

"Jodi said something about Kristin being touched by Vic also."

"That's what she said, but I talked to both of my girls, and they said nothing happened."

"Do your girls know what happened to you?"

"Sure."

"Jodi was trashed when this whole thing came out about Kristin having a dream of being touched by Vic. I don't think it's true."

"Do you still talk to your mom?"

"Oh yeah, sure," she answered almost surprised by the question.

"But she says now because of the case against Vic, she says she shouldn't be talking to me," she chuckled and smiled for the first time. I saw a hint of the old mischievous Meighan I had remembered.

"Is there anything else you want to tell me?" I asked and she shot me a quick and emphatic, "No."

"Right. I'm guessing you don't really want to relive this anymore."

Thinking for a moment, I did have one more question that had always bothered me.

"I always wondered how Tina could have been so friendly with your mom. I mean she was supposed to protect her children as well, and I uh…mean it seems that she stood by and did nothing. How do you guys reconcile that?"

Not even blinking, she instantaneously said, "I don't know."

I tried to press the point further but got stonewalled with a succession of more "I don't knows," clearly not wanting to think or deal with this. We made more small talk about how we needed to keep in touch more, and such. As we hugged, I had a sense of pressing my side against Tina's belly for a polite hug, the last time I had seen her before she died.

As many adult victims of childhood sexual abuse, Meighan had become an accomplished cover up artist. Her emotions and anger were tightly wrapped, emerging only under the cover of inebriation. As she walked away, I was reminded of the way Tina had looked before she died, and I shuddered.

Police Report and the State's Attorney

Police Report and the State's Attorney

In the fall of 2008, Jodi finally summoned the courage to file a report of sexual childhood abuse with the St. Petersburg Police Department. Still living in St. Pete, Janey accompanied her to the police station.

Detective David Wawrzynski was assigned to the case. He appeared to be in his mid to late thirties, of medium build, and in good physical condition. His short-cropped hair had some splashes of gray. After interviewing both sisters, he was convinced they were telling the truth, and wanted to pursue a criminal case against Victor Morgan. The case, however, had multiple legal pitfalls from the start. First, the alleged incidents took place over thirty years ago. The rape victim, Tina, was now deceased, and the crime, if it had been committed, occurred in Lakeland, Polk County, Florida—out of the jurisdiction of the St. Pete PD. The more the detective listened to Jodi's story, however, and the corroboration by her sister, the more he became convinced that Victor Morgan was guilty of child sexual abuse and battery. After months of investigating and interviewing Victor Morgan, Detective David Wawrzynski felt that he had enough evidence to take the complaint to the next level—the Florida State Attorney's office.

Florida State Law makes it mandatory to report childhood sexual abuse. As referenced in section 39.201, F.S., "Any person who knows, or has reasonable cause to suspect, that a child is abused, abandoned, or neglected by a parent, legal custodian, caregiver, or other person responsible for the child's welfare, as defined in this chapter, or that a child is in need of supervision and care and has no parent, legal custodian, or responsible adult relative immediately known and available to provide supervision and care shall report such knowledge or suspicion to the department."

Two significant problems for the Attorney General's office were the obvious huge delay of reporting the crimes here, and two, the above-referenced statute was made law years after the abuse crimes had occurred.

Nonetheless, Jodi, Janey, Pam and I went to local state attorney's office in Clearwater, Florida on April 30, 2009 for interviews. Prior to the meeting, we all had lunch at the Red Mesa Grill in downtown St. Pete. The mood was hopeful but somber. I think in retrospect we all knew that successful prosecution of Victor Morgan was a long shot at best. However, the detective had given us some optimism, albeit interlaced with legal realities. At the meeting, we were interviewed separately and then together. Jodi was first, and after returning to the waiting area, I knew the news was not good.

"They're not going to do a fucking thing," she sobbed, falling into her husband's arms. Next Janey, Jodi, and I met with the two attorneys in one room. I was up next and summoned all of my best arguments, but Maria Miaoulis, the lead state attorney assigned to the case was unimpressed. After she stated all the legal problems with the possible indictment, such as the lapsed time and deceased victim, the accused was old and in poor health, etc., I made one final plea:

"There is a precedence for this you know—John Demjanjuk."

Born in 1920, he is a retired autoworker and former US citizen, who had gained notoriety after being accused of Holocaust–related war crimes. On April 14, 2009, immigration agents began Demjanjuk's deportation, removing him from his home in a wheelchair. He was scheduled to fly to Munich from Cleveland, but the legal order was reversed and another stay granted by the court. On May 7, 2009, the U.S. Supreme Court rejected Demjanjuk's appeal and on May 8, 2009, he was ordered to surrender to U.S. Immigration agents for deportation to Germany. On May 11, Demjanjuk left his Cleveland home by ambulance and was taken to the airport, where he was deported by plane to Germany. He arrived there the next morning on May 12. On July 13, 2009, Demjanjuk was formally charged with 27,900 counts of acting as an accessory to murder, one for each person who died at Sobibor during the time he was accused of serving as a guard at the Nazi death camp.

Although my intention was not to compare Victor Morgan to a Nazi murderer, (although I'm sure some of his victims might argue this point), I wanted to point out that merely age and poor health was not a sufficient reason to drop prosecution of a crime. The state's lawyers acknowledged my argument, but made certain that the sisters understood what would happen to them should this come to trial.

"You will have to tell your stories and relive all of this all over again. His (Victor Morgan's) attorney will seek multiple delays and with his poor health, he might not even survive to the end of a trial. You need to really consider if this is what you want to do. Perhaps just the reality that he has been scared enough to hire an attorney and has to live in fear of prosecution might be enough vindication for you. And suppose we go to trial and we lose. You may end up feeling even worse."

The message was loud and clear: We may believe you, but the legal basis for an arrest and trial are weak and with our limited resources, we must choose our cases carefully. There is a high probability of not winning here. Jodi took the news the hardest—tears falling across her cheeks almost non-stop, hands firmly clenched in her lap. It wasn't that the attorneys didn't believe her—it was judicial reality of an unwinnable litigation.

We all left in dour moods, knowing the likelihood was high that Victor Morgan would never see his day in court, and justice would not be served.

On March 29, 2010, Detective Wawrzynski agreed to speak with me concerning his investigation. We had met about one year ago at the State Attorney's office in Clearwater on April 30, 2009. One month earlier, he had interviewed Victor Morgan in the alleged perpetrator's home.

Before we started I asked for his permission to tape our conversation. He gave an immediate and emphatic, "No."

"Do you think Victor Morgan is guilty of these crimes?" I asked first.

He did not hesitate. "Yes."

"Why is that?"

"When someone is accused of such a terrible crime as this, their immediate reaction is to deny it. He simply said that he could not remember."

"Anything else?"

"Yes. He claimed he was suffering with dementia; however, he had no problem remembering facts before and after the time period of the alleged abuse."

I was not surprised. His assessment certainly fit with my impression of the man. The detective was right—committing sex acts against a child is not something a person forgets, drunk or sober. If one is innocent of such an accusation, the first and most common reaction is to deny it. Selective amnesia is not a believable defense unless, of course, one is guilty. Victor, his wife Helen, and their attorney, all claimed he was suffering from dementia. I had never seen any evidence of confusion or memory loss when I had been around him, so this claim is not one which is believable. As future events would confirm, Victor Morgan is a pathological liar.

"I was a mean drunk," said Victor to me one time at a family picnic, as we watched several of my wife's siblings getting wasted.

"How's that?" I asked.

"I'd rather not say," he answered, and then without a pause changed to another subject. I concluded that his memory of past abuses was far from impaired. He just didn't want to talk about it— afraid to reveal too much to anyone. His way of dealing with it was to submerge any memory back somewhere in his warped brain, convinced perhaps that the only reason his inner monster had been released was because of the demon alcohol.

I continued. "How about the computer you seized from his home? Did you turn up any childhood pornography?"

"No. The hard disc was clean."

"Clean as in empty or having been erased?"

"We couldn't tell, but it doesn't matter," he said.

I nodded my head and tried to refocus by not asking any more dumb questions.

"The family wants to know if they can have the computer back."

"Yes. Just tell them to call me."

"I assumed that since we haven't heard from you since last April, the State Attorney's office had decided not to proceed with their investigation?"

"Yes and no."

"How so?" I asked.

He then slid a piece of paper across the desk for me to view:

IN THE CIRCUIT COURT OF THE SIXTH JUDICIAL CIRCUIT OF THE STATE OF FLORIDA AND FOR PINELLAS COUNTY

F09-02262

STATE OF FLORIDA
v.
VICTOR MORGAN

CHARGE: SEXUAL BATTERY (4 CTS)
OFFICER: DETECTIVE DAVID WAWRZYNSKI
AGENCY: SPPD
OFFENSE NO.   SP08-060684

Assistant State Attorney Maria Miaoulis, having conducted a State Attorney Investigation in the above-styled cause, recommends the filling of a No Information for the following reasons:

Without further independent corroborating evidence the State will be unable to prove these charges beyond a reasonable doubt, as there appears to be jurisdictional issues. In addition, the Statue of Limitations has run on most of the charges.

If your department disagrees with this recommendation, the investigating officer and his supervisor should immediately contact Division Director William A. Loughery or Bruce L. Bartlett, Chief Assistant at 464-6221. For speedy trial purposes, time is of the essence.

The letter was not dated. The detective must have read my mind and said, "I don't know why, but they never put dates on these things."

"So," I said, "It is neither open nor closed?"

"Pretty much. But we would need new evidence to ask for a new hearing." I had anticipated as much.

The statement about "jurisdictional issues," referred to the fact that Tina's alleged rape had occurred in Lakeland, Florida. And the subject about the statute of limitations, as the detective would explain to me, was that the laws had changed over the years. Although currently there are no statues of limitations for sexual abuse on a child under the age of twelve in Florida, the applicable laws default to the time period when the alleged crime had occurred. Thus, in 1979, such an open-ended law was not in effect.

The detective gave me the name of the records secretary and told me to call her if I wanted to see more information about the investigation. He apologized for the brevity of the meeting, but said he was now working in the homicide division, and had to drive across the state to Coco Beach to interview an inmate.

The next day I spoke with Betty Long in the St. Petersburg Police Records Department and provided her with the case number. She found the report and said she could supply me with a copy but it would be a redacted report. Redacted is a legal word for edited. Thus, the only name that would appear in the report was the accused, Victor Morgan. Everyone else's name would be blacked out. Following my interviews, I figured I could guess who was who.

Two days later she called me to say the report was ready. Another trip to the SPPD and $7.25 later, the twenty-one-page report was in my hands. I did not read it until that evening, but since that night, I feel haunted whenever I look at. Following are some excerpts of St. Petersburg Police Department Incident/Investigative Report Case Number 2008-060684. The section titled, "Charges" are described as "BY OVER 18 YOA SEX BATTERY VICTIM UNDER 12 YOA." Of further note in Section 2, the crime description reads, "FORCIBLE SODOMY."

This, as well as several other "facts" recorded in the report, are just wrong. Jodi was the only one to give primary testimony and when I later questioned her about making any statements to the police about "sodomy," she denies doing so.

On page four of the report the "victim," (again presumably Jodi) "stated it is believed that [blank] was sodomized as a child by Victor which led to her abuse of substance and alcohol." The blank most likely refers to Tina and again Jodi denies ever testifying to this.

On page six under the "supplement narrative section" where it is written, "The following will detail efforts to conduct a follow-up investigation related to Saint Petersburg Police Department report #2008-060684. The original involves allegations of forced sexual activity between a birth father, identified as VICTOR MORGAN and his natural daughters." This is not correct since Victor Morgan had two naturial sons, and no daughters.

The report continued, "these allegations allegedly became known and discussed amongst the family after the death of one of the siblings. This matter involves a deathbed declaration by one victim." That victim can only be Tina, and her declaration was not just on her "deathbed." She had told her sisters and me numerous times about the abuse prior to her death. Furthermore, Tina was not a natural daughter.

The report continues, "Several of the listed victims are reluctant to involve themselves with the matter. Each has referred me to speak with [blank] (most likely Meighan) resides in [blank] (Atlanta) and phone contact has been made with her. We have attempted to arrange a phone interview and a confirmed date has not yet been set."

The sisters I spoke with were far from "reluctant to involve themselves with the matter." However, the only true witness to Tina's rape was Meighan, and thus the referral to her name in the report. Meighan confirmed with me that she had later spoken with the St. Pete Police Department. Indeed on page sixteen of the report Meighan's statement corroborates what she told Tina and I later.

From Meighan's testimony to the police is the following statement.

"[Blank] (Meighan) stated MORGAN would call her into a bedroom and would want her to rub his back. She stated he would tell her that 'Mom wanted to make him comfortable.' She advised countless times he would penetrate her vagina with his finger and/or tongue. She added she had no way to estimate how many times this occurred. She added she knew VICTOR MORGAN was touching her sisters, and she stated she would try to get him to touch her instead of them. She advised she would comfort him and try to coax him to leave the other girls alone."

"[Blank] (Meighan) advised she left the house at age fifteen and went to live with her father. She stated MORGAN would often say he was going to kill her mother. She added she remembered one occasion when MORGAN held a shotgun on all of the kids. She stated this happened in the home in Shore Acres. She added the physical and sexual contact occurred in all of the homes where the family lived together."

I don't want to imply that the investigation was botched. However, the incorrect usage of the accusation of sodomy by Jodi, the misstatement of Tina's "deathbed confession," and the gender error in describing Victor Morgan's natural children, casts dubious suspicion about the strength of the case presented to the State's Attorney office.

Thus, I am left troubled by what might have been. Suppose it had been Tina, the actual rape victim, who went to the police before she died and filed the complaint. Knowing her as I did, I don't think she was as strong as Jodi, and was too far along in her addiction pattern to take this action. Would the results have been different? What if I had pushed her more to go to the police and file a complaint, rather than staying mired in my own denial? Would she have even listened to me? I don't know if it would have been different. All I know for certain is that the criminal justice system failed this family miserably despite calls from the children for help on multiple occasions. And therein lies one of the greatest tragedies of the Ackerson-Morgan clan unit, and of many similar families where incest and abuse are the unspoken norm.

Pam

We had only fifteen minutes before the start of the questioning by the state's attorney's office. It was April 30, 2009 in Clearwater, Florida. Sitting on an old marble bench, the strong sunlight splashed through the floor to ceiling glass, making it difficult for me to see her face. Pam, the oldest, and probably most successful sister, had gotten out of her childhood home before the hellishness had started in full throttle. Pam had a child out of wedlock as a teenager. Later her first husband died in a construction accident. She finally remarried years later to Elliot Barden, an Ob/Gyn doctor in Polk County, Florida. Pam went to nursing school and later became a nurse anesthetist. Elliot gave up the obstetrical part of his practice in the 1990's when the medical malpractice premiums for delivering babies got absurdly high in Florida. They relocated to Lee County and now live in a country-Key West style home near Ft. Myers.

"The pain I feel is acute and the guilt, more so. You see, as the oldest, I should have known and protected them—that's my burden. Intellectually I know that's BS—but in my heart, well that's another matter." Shifting her weight a bit, she said she was quite anxious to talk before the state's attorney and David Wawrszynski, the St. Petersburg Police Detective, could interview us. Short and heavy-set, but still in good shape, Pam was the closest to me in age and the oldest of the Ackerson daughters.

"When did you first know or suspect that abuse was occurring in your family?"

"Knew or suspected?"

"Either one."

"I had always suspected something terrible was happening, but it wasn't until our first family reunion in Dunnellon, when Tina started to talk with the other sisters." Her rounded face, framed by curls of black hair, suddenly caught some sunlight. I saw the same flat, almost expressionless and serious gaze that I noted with her other sisters, but with a slight twinkle in her eyes. I decided to switch gears.

"Ok, let's go back earlier if we can. When did you first move out from your mom and dad's home?"

That she answered immediately.

"It was after their divorce…I think April of 1970. Mom and Vic had gotten married in 1967, so I had spent three years with them. Although I was sent away, you know, as I had had a baby. That was uh, '68, and I came back in '69." She seemed very intent upon getting her dates correct. I recalled Tina telling me she had her first child, born out of wedlock, was later adopted.

"The few years you were with them, was there a lot of drinking going on?"

"Constant. At first it was kind of a novelty since our parents were social drinkers, and we had never heard my parents fighting. So when Mom and Vic started to fight openly in front of us, we all thought it was kind of funny. But then as time went on, they established a pattern, and this was everyday. They would get up at noon, start drinking cheap Scotch, and by dinner, they were loopy, and after dinner, they were obnoxious, and then the fighting and yelling started."

"Okay. Getting back to the first family reunion, I guess I kind of have a blank about that. What do you remember Tina saying?"

"She just started talking about it, and about that same time the younger ones started talking amongst themselves. Like Jodi didn't know about Meighan. But I don't recall exactly what she said. Yet from there forward, it was a constant conversation amongst us."

"Can you remember any details?"

She paused for a moment, concentrating as her dark eyes focused on me.

"It was when Elliot, (her husband,) and I were living in Winter Haven, and Meighan was over. She started talking about the deal she made with Vic. You know about that, right?"

"The deal was Vic could do anything he wanted to her but he had to leave Mary and Jodi alone."

"Yes."

"And Mary came up and talked about it as well."

"So when was the first time that anyone actually challenged your mother about this?"

"It was just last fall with Jodi finally going to the police. Jodi called Mom and told her, and Mom called her a liar. Jodi got upset, started to cry and then called me. I called Mom and told her that she was wrong, and she didn't know anything about what happened, because she was drunk all the time. I told her then what had happened to Tina."

"Can you tell me about that?"

"It had to have happened in the house at West White Oak Drive in Lakeland, so Tina would have to have been oh ten, eleven, or twelve, because I was there in 1969 or 1970. I was there and remember the house was dark, so Mom and Vic must have gone to bed. I was still up and Tina came to me—it was like two or three in the morning. The kitchen light was on, so it was like ambient light. She was obviously upset, crying and shaking, and told me Vic had touched her, and to not tell Mom."

"Did she say she had been raped?"

Her face grimaced a bit as she thought, and chose her words slowly. "I was seventeen at the time, and I could not imagine an adult doing that kind of thing to a child." A tear began to form in one eye. "Bud, (her older brother), was still at home and hadn't left for the military yet. Since Dad had left, he was kind of our protector, you know. Well I talked to Bud, and maybe Tina did, and he said he would take care of it. He was always ready for a fight with Vic. Anyway, after that night, I don't think he ever touched her again."

Two attorneys sharply dressed in dark suits walked by us, chatting with a thin younger woman in a stylish black and white outfit. Their shoes clicked loudly on the stone floor, making it harder for me to hear Pam. So, I leaned closer.

"I truly believe Bud said something to Vic, because the little girls, (Mary, Meighan, and Jodi,) later told me that Vic had told them if they said anything bad about him to Mom, he would kill her."

"You mean he would kill your mother?"

She nodded slowly. "And that's why I think we never heard anything more about all of this business until much later. I think Vic moved from Tina to the other girls, and they never said anything because they were really afraid he would hurt Mom. They of course had seen him beat her before."

I sighed. "Ok, anything else?"

"I'm just learning about the horrible conditions they lived in and the guilt I feel is overwhelming. I bailed, Bud bailed, Chip and Sue all bailed," her voice just trailed off. "We just never knew. Like I just found out that Bobby and X. slept under the kitchen table. I mean like every night. Can you believe it?" I could see the pain and guilt in her face and body. She felt responsible for what had happened, and of course she was not. The sadness in her eyes was unmistakable. I couldn't help but say something. "You weren't the parent. It's wasn't your fault." It seemed to provide a modicum of relief to her, she sighed, shoulders heaving a bit, and as she leaned forward we hugged.

I couldn't say anything, so I just nodded and turned off the recorder.

"So when am I going to meet Denise? (My present wife whom I had married in 2006), I hear she's lovely."

"Soon. We go to Miami a lot to see my grandson, so maybe we'll stay over with you guys one night in Ft. Myers." I glanced at my watch—it was time to meet the detective and the state's attorney.

"It's two o'clock. Let's see how all of this will play out."

I kept struggling to close the lid on that damn box which contained this chapter of my life, and it didn't seem as if I was any closer to shutting it. The cover, or the box, was still warped.

Sue

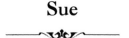

The Rainbow Rivers Club in Dunnellon, Florida was the site of the 2008 Ackerson family reunion. Located at the confluence of the Rainbow and Withlacoochee Rivers, the clear waters are fed by natural springs arising out of Florida's ancient limestone, and remains a constant 72 degrees year-round. I had mixed feelings about attending another family event of Tina's family, but felt it was important for Emily to stay in touch with her relatives. The three of us had been there before as a family, and I knew the setting well—old Florida with lots of oaks, pines, bald cypress, heat, and bugs. After a barbeque and lots of drinking, Emily disappeared to visit with her cousins. I sat in the small wood cabin with a window air conditioner humming and stared blankly at the television. It was dusk, and I was not feeling social. Sue knocked on my door and came in to talk. An old fan whirled around, as we sat on the screened outside porch in two rocking chairs. Being November, the stifling Florida humidity was just starting to break. We had previously talked about my interviewing her, and she had readily agreed. However, we never seemed to be able to connect on a time. The reunion seemed ideal and thus another motivation for me to show up.

With her beaming smile and high apple cheeks, Sue looked so much like Tina, they could have easily been mistaken for twins. Yet she also had a lot of her mother's Pollyanna personality trait. As I asked her about growing up amidst the chaos and abuse of her stepfather, she would repeatedly deflect, minimize, and change the subject. As with her sisters, she would often forget details and locations and events. As I reflected on the magnitude of the dysfunctional home life, it seemed like the same record being played over and over again. One of the hallmarks of post-traumatic stress disorder is avoidance of the subject and emotional numbing. This leads to the distance and detachment I felt while interviewing the other sisters. The human mind tries to protect itself by purposefully forgetting the painful events, much like a computer deleting corrupted files.

"I think I am responsible for Tina's death—some of the sisters and I talked about a possible intervention—you know like getting her admitted again to a hospital or rehab. We never did, and I guess she and Billy decided to hasten their exit."

Dropping my interviewing role for a moment I reassured her. "I don't think that would have made any difference. You know she had been in and out of the finest rehab facilities several times. You shouldn't blame yourself for this. It's simply not the truth."

Choking back some tears, she nodded and continued on about the day her younger sister had died.

"Janey and I tried to reach her several times that night, and I was getting irritated with her for not being available at such a time." She was referring to her brother, Bobby dying of a drug overdose just three days before. Tina was well aware of it—having called me the day of his death, leaving a sobbing voicemail on my home phone.

I knew then that she had no concept of her sister's disease or how advanced it had become. I had lived through the alcoholic's divorcing themselves from the lives and needs of loved ones too many times. Sue clearly did not get it yet. Her animated voice and always-optimistic tone continued.

"We went to sleep that night and woke up to a phone call that Bobby Tribou, (Janey's brother-in-law), had taken Bobby Ackerson's truck without permission right after Bobby had died. It ran out of gas and was later found abandoned on US 19, (a major highway in the county). Janey was furious at her brother-in-law because she had just learned that he had provided the lethal mix of drugs that had killed her twin brother only days before. Anyway, I kept having this nagging feeling to see if Tina was okay."

"We arrived at her condo, and when I felt the doorknob open I knew that she was dead. I walked in with Janey behind me. There was a half wall on the left. That's when I saw Tina's feet and Janey fell to the ground sobbing."

"There was a staged single glass of wine on the counter."

"How did you know it was staged?"

"I just thought it was strange because it looked arranged."

I didn't recall seeing it when I had entered the condo.

"What happened next?"

"I called 911 to report her death. Then the phone rang and it was Billy calling from the beach, he said Tina was going to the beach. I told him that was impossible because she was dead. He didn't say anything—just hung up the phone. I couldn't touch her."

"Then Mom came over and the police and ambulance. A black and white checkered cab drove up and Billy got out with coke-circled nostrils and was just standing there strung out. I'd never liked him. I remember when we were young he spilled flaming liquor on Tina's bare chest. That's when we decided to call you because it just didn't seem right—you know—with Billy there and Tina dead. You know he died two years later of the same thing as Tina, right?"

I nodded.

Her usually bubbly face turned cold and expressionless. I wasn't used to seeing her sad or mournful—it just wasn't her style. She had gained some weight since I had last seen her and she began to shift uncomfortably in a creaky wooden rocking chair. Cicada bugs chirped noisily outside.

"For six months I cried so deeply and checked out from everyone and everything except for my savior on earth, Pat, (her husband), and my boys." The family had been raised Catholic, and Sue had been one of the more religious ones of her siblings.

She wanted to switch gears and a few moments later Sue started to speak about the few things she remembered growing up.

"I was sick after hearing all that stuff about Vic."

"Did he ever abuse you?"

"No."

"Did you ever witness him abusing your brothers or sisters?"

"No."

"In retrospect, Dad and Jeannie, (her stepmother), were delayed in getting the kids out of the house. But you know that if anyone visited, they would clean up their act, and everything would appear— well you know, like normal. When I was young I truly believed that I had a healthy childhood. That is until Victor."

Her hands were clenched tightly on her lap and I could see she was becoming restless and fidgety.

"I remember the house in the orange grove, (Lakeland). It was so remote, the smell of the orange blossoms so thick it would make you want to puke."

I thought that was an odd description since I had always loved the way the orange blossoms had smelled in the Florida springtime.

But I could see how if it was really intense one could have that reaction. But then I thought again and no—that wasn't it. I suspected it was the association of the smell with what must have been happening in her family life at the time, since that was about the time of Tina's rape. I don't think she connected the two.

"Uprooted from St. Pete, it was such a strange place. Pam and I shared an office with glass French doors. I would cry myself to sleep nightly with Mom and Vic's drunken screams in the background. It really disgusted me to see the gallon bottles of cheap wine and vodka. And there was Mom naked and screaming and crying. It was not a pretty site."

"Do you remember anything about Tina saying she had been raped by Vic?"

"No. I guess she told Pam that. I didn't learn of that until a few years before her death."

This seemed to fit with the story given by both Pam and Janey.

"I don't remember a whole lot about my youth. (More memory files deleted.) I do know that I left home when I was 16 to get away from both Vic and Jeannie. I left for self-preservation and slept under a bridge, until I was taken in by a friend's family."

Not too much later, she would move in with her boyfriend Pat Callahan, from St. Petersburg. They would live together for the next twelve years, and finally got married in Sedona, Arizona when she was 28 years old. They would have two boys, Sean and Brian. The diverging paths of both boys tells a lot about the insidious addiction gene passed along from one generation to the next.

Sean was a tall, thin, and handsome boy who at first excelled in school. However, in high school he began to smoke a lot of marijuana and his grades began to slip. As with most heavy weed users his motivation for school or work was near zero, and he barely graduated from college. He would hold odd jobs and talk about joining the Air Force, but never did. As the nationwide economic slump widened in 2008, his ability to find work in the small town of Dunnellon, Florida, did not become any easier. Ultimately he fathered a child, Lillie, with another girl who became addicted to Oxycontin painkillers. In early 2010, she was arrested for theft and falsification of Pawn broker laws. At the time of this writing, Sean is finally clean and sober, still living with Sue and Pat, but working full-time in a tire shop. Sue and Pat have filed for custody of Lillie.

Brian, on the other hand, had a whole other set of problems. He was born with spina bifida, a birth defect in which the backbone and spinal canal do not close before birth. Despite multiple correction surgeries, he has never been able to walk or have complete bowel and bladder control. Sue was, and is, a great mother. Tina had told me she thought Brian had been given to Sue to mother because "God knew no one else could take care of him as well as she." He is confined to a wheelchair and will never walk. However, he has a good mind and did well in school. So well in fact, that in July 2010 he began school for a Video Editing Degree at St. Petersburg College.

"Did you ever live with your Dad?"

"Yes, but only for about six months. Jeannie was almost as bad as Vic?"

"In what way?"

"Drunk and stupid all the time."

"What else?"

"I quit school when I was in the 11th grade, but later got my GED, and went to SPJC, (St. Petersburg Junior College). My grades weren't great, but I did get a degree."

She works as a consultant for old and new nuclear power plant facilities, having obtained postgraduate training in health physics and radiation protection. She inspects them and makes sure they are safe to open, or re-open after a shutdown. Hence her decision to live in Dunnellon, which is close to the Crystal River Nuclear Power Plant, one of Florida's two nuclear power plant facilities.

Her eyes turned downward as she reflected. "I often wonder where I would be if I had been nurtured as a child. I'd probably have gotten a bachelor's or master's degree. Who knows?"

"Do you remember your grandmother?"

"Yes. She was such a strong woman. I have horrible guilt because of leaving that monster, (Vic), with grandma and the little kids. I didn't speak to my mother for two years after I left home. All I remember was fighting with Vic and dumping his booze out, and him popping oysters off the canal sea wall and eating them—gross!"

"Any more thoughts about your Mom and her role in all of this?"

"Why she stayed with Vic nobody knows. Perhaps an already failed marriage, fear of being alone, growing old without anyone…

or having to face the fact that all of us were forever scarred by him, and if she actually did anything, she would have to acknowledge what really had happened." She was however one of the few sisters who maintained contact with her mother.

I let her pause for a bit and then asked, "Any other thoughts or memories you can share?"

She thought for a moment and then said, "I dreamt about Bobby. He was handsome and green-eyed and his normal weight; not the big beer belly he would always pat with pride. He was in a plaid flannel shirt and jeans and in a lovely small house with an atrium. He started walking down a walkway and all of these people started to walk and follow him. He looked so happy and peaceful. At the end of the walkway was a ticket counter where he asked for tickets to a show. It was like he was telling me he was really okay now. It made me happy."

"I still haven't dreamt about Tina. I grieve her still. This life is so sad."

I didn't press her for anymore, in part because there seemed little else to add and in part because I couldn't take any more stories. I had started to become numb to the horrors and the sadness myself. Months later, as I lit a memorial candle on the sixth anniversary of her death, January 8, 2010, I too had plenty of what ifs left unanswered.

Bobby

Tina would describe her younger brother, Bobby, as a time bomb—ready to explode at anytime. All of the abused sisters whom I interviewed were convinced Victor had sodomized him, although none had ever directly witnessed the act. Every interaction I had with Robert Ackerson confirmed his self described label as the "black sheep" of the family, and no one's life epitomized better than Bobby's, the devastating affects of childhood physical abuse and sexual molestation. Abusing alcohol and drugs at a young age, he was finally sober for several years when he met, and later married, his future wife Jeanice.

It was a bright sparkling fall day in October when I met Jeanice Bunday at a Starbucks in Lakeland, Florida. I sipped warm green tea and she indulged in a large iced caloric coffee creation with whip cream.

"I don't order these very often," she said after we hugged, apologizing for her treat.

"How's Bobby doing?" I asked, referring to her troubled son.

"He's in the National Guard in Kuwait, but may be coming back soon. I told him he couldn't live with Todd (her second husband) and I again. He's okay while he's in the military, but when he gets home he hangs with the wrong crowd, and then he'll start drinking and drugging again."

She shifted a bit in the outside black wrought iron chair. The pain of her son's life was clearly visible.

"Perhaps the military is the best place for him," I said.

"Yeah, that's what I think too. His tour is up soon and he may re-enlist. He talks about going to Afghanistan so he can shoot someone legally."

That wasn't as odd a statement to me as it might seem to someone who didn't know Robert Ackerson, Jr. Even at a young age, it was easy to predict his future would be troubled and violent. When our daughter, Emily, was only one and a half, and "little Bobby" as he was known, was three, we were at Meighan's house for a party. There was a screened-in porch area, and all of the kids were playing with a ball there. As any parent, I had one eye on my child, and one on the adults in the living room, then I heard Emily start to cry. Little Bobby had her pinned facedown on the river rock gravel, and was stepping on her head. I will never forget the look in his eyes—it wasn't fear or anger—it was enjoyment. I sprang forward grabbing him by the collar, hauling the little demon off our crying toddler. Tina scooped Emily up in her arms comforting her, and inspecting her for injuries. As I continued to drag the little demon across the floor to his father, the look in his eyes were soulless, and without remorse. It was as if he had no idea he had done anything wrong. I quickly explained to his father what had happened, and he took over.

"If I ever see you doing that to a little baby again, I will break every bone in your body," Bobby screamed at his son's face, like a drill seargent. Most little boys would cower or cry, but not this one—he just stared into his father's eyes, almost challenging him to go ahead and try it.

I returned to my wife and daughter making sure she wasn't hurt.

"Someday he'll be on a tower or somewhere shooting a gun at innocent people," I prophesized.

"He's just being a little boy," Tina said to me in denial. I knew there was a river of pain and violence that had seeded inside of the child's psyche even at this young age.

Jeanice had already told me she wasn't sure she could help me very much, but I pushed on.

"While you were married to Bobby did he talk about the abuse he suffered as a child?"

"He admitted to some, but I think he really just kept it stuffed inside," she said, sipping her brown drink. I was certain her hair had been dyed black to cover the gray, and I noted she had not gained much weight since the last time I had seen her, about seven years ago. There were some circles under her eyes, and she seemed tired—not surprising as she worked full-time, was trying to get a second job to make ends meet, and got up with her husband Todd at four-thirty every morning before he went to his job maintaining grounds at a golf course.

"Did he ever go into any details? I asked.

"No, umm," she answered. "I talked to him a couple of times and we went to marital counseling before we divorced and he started to say some stuff, then he locked up, tearing, and then stood up saying, 'This is bullshit! I can't do this and I won't do this.' He kept it inside but I always thought something had happened to him because of his actions."

"So what was he talking about during the counseling?" I continued.

"Oh just how bad his childhood was, you know, and the divorce, but he would never go into details. But I know something happened—I just knew it."

I shifted gears a bit, asking, "So what led to your divorce?"

She didn't hesitate in her answer. "He was verbally, mentally, and physically abusive. I took the first hit and beating and the second one—no."

"Did you have any idea of his abusive behavior before you got married?" I asked.

"No—not at all. Because he was sober when we got married. I told him I wouldn't marry him if he was drinking, and he had been sober for four years. But he had that alcoholic disease, and I think Bobby (her son) is heading down that same path too if he's not careful," she added without prompting.

"Right. He probably has that inherited gene, you know," I said trying to soften any guilt she might be having.

"Oh I know that," she said. "My father was an alcoholic but he was never abusive—had a steady job and provided for his family. He put food on the table, and was never verbally, physically, or sexually abusive towards me."

"I think kids who are abused tend to become abusers themselves because that is all they know," I said.

"Oh I wouldn't doubt that," she said, "because Bobby's temper is every bit as bad as his Dad's. His father just kept things bottled up for so long and then he would explode."

"So he never provided you with any details?" I asked. Her answer was surprising.

"No not really, but he told me he had been in a full body cast when he was young."

"Wow," I said. "That's pretty bad. I never heard that one before."

"Yeah. I'm not even sure that it really happened."

I doubted the veracity of this story and then remembered how much and how often Bobby would lie and exaggerate about things and events.

Oddly I noticed the same expressionless face on Jeanice that the Ackerson daughters had shown me. I was confronting yet another victim of post-traumatic stress, who had submerged her feelings and pain so deep, that the surface seemed lake-like, or becalmed.

I persisted. "What did he say during that counseling session?"

"I always had that gut feeling that he had been abused in more than one way. He told the counselor he had been abused but refused to give any details. We had only one counseling session and he would not go back."

It was obvious to me that he had gotten close to that emotional flame, and was not going back to get burned again.

I was coming up blank, so tried one last question.

"Were there ever any hints in your sexual relations that something had happened to him a child?"

"No. Not unless he opened up to his girlfriend—you know he had an affair when I was three months pregnant with Bobby. But he sure didn't open up to me," she said with a soft giggle.

"Of all his sisters and brothers, who do you think he was closest to?"

She didn't hesitate in her answer. "Tina."

"Really?" I answered. "I would have thought Janey, (his twin sister)."

"No. She moved away with Dick when she was seventeen. He always talked about Janey a lot, but he and Tina were the closest."

I had always wondered about Tina and Bobby's relationship and why it had been so close, and why she had always stuck up for him when no else did, or loaned him money and gave him spare jobs when he was down. They were kindred spirits—both abused—in physical, verbal, emotional, and sexual ways—unprotected by their mother or natural father. During her short life, Tina had succeeded outwardly where Bobby had failed, but in the end, their paths would meet in the cruelest of ironies. He died of a drug overdose on her birthday January 5, 2004, and she of alcoholic induced liver failure only three days later.

I did not press Jeanice for any more because there was nothing more to learn. Tina had told me Bobby had confessed to her he had been a victim of Vic's sodomy, and I doubted any other living person could verify that other than Vic—and he wasn't talking.

"Good luck with Bobby," I said as we hugged. I walked her to a well-worn white Japanese compact. A large black Harley motorcycle engine roared into the cool cloudless air.

"Thanks," she said. "We will all need it."

As I drove away back towards I-4 and Tampa, I remembered the last time I had actually spoken with Bobby—it was just after his divorce and he called our house asking to speak with Tina. His speech was slow and slurred.

"Is Tina there?" he asked.

"No, she's at an AA meeting. Can I give her a message?"

Long pause and muffled tears, "No...not really...just tell her I'm really fucked up...I need to talk to her sometime...and...okay?"

"Sure Bobby," I said. "Take care."

She would always call him back, trying to talk him into sobriety. No matter how much he failed or screwed up she was always there for him. She would bear his pain and not judge him like the rest of the family. I recalled them going to AA meetings together for a while until he fell "off of the wagon."

Childhood physical and sexual abuse is like a festering wound or abscess. Until it is lanced and drained the emotional infection and poison rages on, destroying the mind, the spirit, and ultimately the body. Neither Bobby nor Tina could rid themselves of the suppressed anger and like a virus it would touch and spread to all of their family members and everyone close to them. In the end, that is the tragedy of childhood abuse and incest—it reaches beyond the victim to other loved ones who do not understand, and can never fully know, the horrendous injury it can inflict. Knowledge and action are the only keys to healing so that the abuse cycle does not keep repeating and recreating itself.

There is no "cure" for this injury, but there is hope for survival in a meaningful way if it is recognized early and positive therapeutic steps are taken. Otherwise, as the story of my family shows, the end results are fatal.

A Day at the Beach

Victor Morgan would often drive to the Pinellas County beaches, portable oxygen for his emphysema, in tow. He would like to say he was just going "to bump around." One of the beaches he frequented was a beach at Gandy Boulevard on old Tampa Bay, also known as "bend over beach" since it was known that gays met there to "hook up." October 9, 2009 was probably one of his more eventful outings. After returning home, he started to bleed quite heavily from his rectum, and needed to go to the hospital. The explanation he would later give his wife and healthcare providers was consistent, but implausible. He stated that while at the beach he needed to move his bowels and was quite constipated. So he went into the bushes, found a large stick and tried to disimpact himself. In so doing he tore, or lacerated his bowel. As fantastic as the story seemed, according to Helen's daughters, their mother actually bought his explanation.

He required surgery to repair the torn segment of bowel, and spent longer than a normal amount of time on a ventilator, (breathing machine), and also developed kidney failure. After his operation, which involved examining his rectum and colon while under anesthesia, and then repairing the tear and creating a colostomy, I spoke with his surgeon.

"So if he was trying to relieve himself of his constipation, you probably found a lot of stool in his bowel?" I asked.

"Actually, no," he replied.

I did not need to ask more than that. His rectum may have been instrumented, but it was probably not by him and not to relieve a fecal impaction. The irony of the "accident" was not lost on any of the sisters however. Several of them told me they had never laughed so hard or so long in their entire lives. Indeed, as surreal as the whole event seemed, it did serve a karmic justice.

Emergency room doctors have long been amazed and amused by what people allow others, or perhaps themselves, to insert into their rectums. I have personally seen everything from light bulbs, wrenches, screwdrivers, and scissors to yes, even gerbils. Reportedly, the largest object removed from a person's rectum was a bowling pin. Select subsets of the population find this to be, or at least have been told it is, sexually stimulating. I suspect some people feel that other than a flexible colonoscope, or a digital prostate exam, the rectum should serve as an exit, and not an entry point. Lined with smooth muscle, the rectum and colon, or large bowel, is however very distensible and therefore able to accommodate objects many times its diameter. The muscle is highly vascular, meaning fed by many arteries and veins, so if injured the bleeding can be diffuse and life-threatening. But make no mistake about it—even in the hands of a skilled doctor with a patient under anesthesia, perforation, or tearing of the bowel, is a rare, but known complication of colonoscopy. When it occurs, it is often a catastrophic event, requiring immediate surgery and often, at least temporarily, creation of a colostomy.

We are only left to speculate what exactly was placed into Victor Morgan's rectum that day. With his age, heart and lung problems, the mere fact that he survived the surgery was quite remarkable.

The Fall of a Beautiful Woman

———— ⟨ଓ⟩ ————

By Emily Mokotoff

"I hope you dance." This song, by country singer Leann Womack, blared from my mother's silver Mercedes sedan every time she picked me up from dance, which was every single day of the week. We were stopped at a stoplight and she said, "Emily, I hope you dance. Always. No matter what. Please whatever you do, don't stop dancing, at least for me."

My whole life I knew my mother was always on my side, my biggest fan. From the time I was born until I was nine-years-old, she was my main support and best friend who gave me an amazing, fun-filled childhood. She was that mom who never missed a practice, show, or competition. I could take comfort in the fact that she would always be there no matter what the circumstances because our love was so strong. However, in March 2001, she fell back into an uncontrollable, dangerous journey of alcoholism. No longer did I see my best friend at every dance practice and competition, but rather the shadow of a person who I used to call Mom.

Before alcohol possessed my mother's life, she was an incredibly beautiful, happy, and generous human being who loved her family more than anything. Everything she did was to benefit other people, especially me. She donated her free time to tutoring underprivileged kids at a local school called Academy Prep while also donating computers to the school. Continuing to help out others, she donated money to local art and theatre centers around the area. Because of all her honorable work she was well known and respected through out the community.

Being my mother's only daughter, I meant the world to her. I can remember her telling me throughout my childhood, "Seltzer is my drink of choice." I had never seen her drink anything else. I took pride in that fact and would brag to my friends saying, "My mother hasn't ever even drank a glass of wine!" Well this wasn't true because right after I was born my mother started drinking. Noticing this problem, she went to rehab and was essentially cured. She didn't pick up any sort of alcohol for six years.

During my spring break in 2001, we went on our annual skiing trip to Big Sky, Montana. This trip was different than the other ones. We were out to eat at a nice steak diner, when my mom took my dad's glass of wine. Filled with fear, my dad anxiously asked, "Tina what are you doing?" "Just one sip, David. I'll be fine." That one sip was what set off her path of destruction for the next three years. I had never seen my mother even touch alcohol, and now here she was in front of me taking just one sip of wine. I was shocked and confused because of my dad's reaction. "Why was he so scared?" I thought. This one sip changed the happy and generous person my mother once was and turned her into a destructive, selfish creature that seemingly didn't care about anyone. Her change was most noticeable in her support and love for my dancing.

I performed a ballet solo to Braham's Lullaby at a local competition called "I Love Dance" in St. Petersburg, Florida. When awards were being announced, I won first place in my category and was chosen to continue to nationals in Las Vegas and to participate in their program called Junior and Senior Sweethearts and Heartthrobs. This was a distinct and prestigious honor. I immediately cleared my summer schedule and accepted this opportunity.

I arrived in Sin City in the dead of summer 2001. I can remember sitting patiently in the window seat, waiting to get off the four-hour flight, and looking out to see the infamous Vegas Strip amongst a barren land. To participate both in the national competition and the I Love Dance program, I had to survive in Vegas for three long weeks. My mom accompanied me for the first two weeks until my dad could come out to meet us and watch me compete and perform. Fear electrified my body. At home, she would be drunk 24/7. There wasn't one moment in the day where she wouldn't be slurring her words, stumbling around, and looking like a complete mess. I hoped with all my heart that she could be sober for this trip and not an embarrassment like she usually was.

Rehearsals ran extremely late for Junior/Senior Sweethearts and Heartthrobs not ending sometimes until 3 a.m. I yearned for the comfort of my mother to help me relax and encourage me to stay strong; however, I didn't have this once in my three weeks in Vegas. Every time I would come back to the room, I would find that it reeked of cheap wine with a passed out, drunk mother already asleep on the bed. One night I didn't have the room key. I used a hotel phone, anxiously praying that someone would answer. After three tries I got nothing. Everyone had already left and I was all alone. I quickly ran to our room and knocked and knocked on the door, but no answer. Physically and emotionally exhausted, I collapsed outside the room.

Somehow with all this external stress, I ended up winning 3rd place nationally for my ballet solo. I felt so accomplished yet saddened at the same time. Just a year ago my mother would've felt even happier and prouder than I was, but now she was different and had different priorities. I had been replaced with bottles of wine and booze. The mother I had known for nine years kept slipping away and each day I would fall asleep filled with anxiety wondering if she'd still be alive in the morning.

Throughout the next two years, two more notable events occurred involving my mother's newfound neglect. Dance competitions were located all over the state, though mainly in Tampa, Orlando, and Lakeland. In the past, driving to dance competitions had been a positive, exciting experience for my mother and me. We were both so anxious yet pumped at the same time for the future events that would ensue. We had to be in Lakeland by 3 o' clock, which meant we needed to leave by one at the latest. I walked downstairs to see what was happening because I hadn't seen my mother since the morning. The site I encountered was horrifying. Her designer clothes were falling off her body. Her hair looked as if it hadn't been washed in days. It was greasy, pulled back into a tight ponytail, and her normally red-dyed hair was showing grey roots, which was something she never let happen when she was sober. I called her out of the room, "Mom? We need to go soon." She stumbled out and slammed face first into the door, then fell on the ground.

My entire body was shaking. It was vital that I get to this competition on time because there were set times when we would compete. I didn't know what to do. She was in such a state that she didn't know who she was, where she was, or even what day it was. In a panic, I did the only thing I could think to do. I called my father, a full-time doctor. The phone rang and he answered as he always does. At first I couldn't even speak I was crying so hard. "Calm down Em, what's going on?" he asked. "It's Mom again. I have to be in Lakeland in two hours and she can barely stand on her own two feet. I don't know how I'm going to get there and I really want to compete, Dad.

I've been practicing all year." Thinking of solutions he asked, "Alright, well is there anyone else that can take you that hasn't left yet." I responded saying, "No, everyone's already left and I don't have any of the Mom's numbers." Doing the only thing he could do, my dad left the hospital immediately to drive me out to Lakeland. Up to that point in my life, I had never felt so much disappointment and fear. All the other times I could think of ways to excuse my mother's drunken actions, but this one felt like a knife in my heart. She used to love driving me to competitions and now I was beginning to realize she really wasn't there. The drive up with my dad was completely silent; neither of us said a word. She was slowly dismantling not only her life, but also my father's and mine.

The last straw came at my dance recital. My mother's alcoholism turned my father and me into constant babysitters. In a time where I was supposed to be parented, I turned into the parent trying to help my mother grow up and become an adult again. Our dance recitals were the culmination of a year of dance. I was in about eight numbers, so I couldn't play babysitter that night. During the performance, my mother had been sitting with my father and all our family like she was supposed to. She had driven separately and after the performance, was nowhere to be found. We knew she was there, her car was at the theatre, but no one knew where she was. During the performance before intermission, a woman who we did not know somehow found my dad amongst a dark audience and asked, "Sir, is this your wife? I can't play babysitter anymore." My mom was completely smashed at my very important performance, a thing she would never even dare to do just two years ago. After the show, I found my parents, but I did not know what had happened yet. After all the "Congratulations" and "You were beautiful up there," I got in the car with my dad and he told me what had happened. "We should just call the police on her. She's operating a vehicle right now." We both watched her driving in front of us for about another thirty seconds then my dad said, "Jesus, I can't do that and put her in jail. She's driving perfectly." During these years, she was able to re-learn how to function completely drunk in daily life. She had officially become another person, one whose body was always consuming and possessed by alcohol.

Over a three-year period of time, she was admitted to rehab six different times and detox three times. After the second stint in rehab,

I was hopeful and optimistic because day after day she continued to be sober. Finally, she was back; the demon of alcohol had left my mother's heart, body, and mind. Even though I was still resentful for the past years, I wanted so much to believe that this was true and she had conquered her addiction. She became reliable again; I could trust her to be there to pick me up and be at dance practices again.

I woke up for school one day; however, this day was different than most. It was going to be the third month that my mother was sober, a very significant period of time, according to Alcoholics Anonymous. While eating breakfast I went up to her, hugged her, and exclaimed, "Mom, I am so proud of you! Today is three months. You've accomplished so much." Instead of reciprocating my excitement she smirked slightly and said, "Yeah, thanks." Her reaction scared me because I thought she'd be excited about her sobriety. I suddenly had a very bad feeling in my stomach. After school I came home and needed to check on my mom. I walked in the front door and yelled, "Mom, Mom...Mom?" There was no reaction. I searched the entire upstairs in the bedroom, kitchen, living room, but I couldn't find her. I hesitantly and slowly walked downstairs, scared of what I would find. "Mom?" I called one more time, and found her in the downstairs kitchen, back to her old ways and clearly intoxicated. With glassy eyes, greasy hair, and a deviant smile she asked, "Hoowww waaasss... schoool, sweetie?" Her slurred words were all I needed to hear. I could feel the anger rising from my toes, to my stomach, and exploding out through my head. "How could you do this? You couldn't give me at least three months of sobriety? This was such an important day. How could you do this?" The new, positive light I had put on my mother got thrown into a dark, frustrated place of hatred. I couldn't wrap my mind around how she could be so selfish and completely abandon me.

My mother's condition was much more serious than other alcoholics. She suffered from Hepatitis C, a disease that affects the liver. With the amount of alcohol she consumed in conjunction with this disease, her blood had no way to filter through the liver due to how much alcohol it was already trying to process. Every time I saw her in the ICU, she was yellow due to this liver disease. Doctors kept telling her, "One more drink and that's it, Tina. Your liver simply cannot handle it." Like a typical addict, nothing, not even death stood in the way of her and those bottles of white Woodridge wine. After she got out of the hospital, I sat her down one night after dinner. "Mom you really need to stop what you're doing. Out of anyone in this world I want you to be there for my Bat Mitzvah, to be there to walk me down the aisle, and be there to see my children being born. At the rate you're at you won't be here for any of it." I thought bringing up these huge milestones in my life would make her understand the severity of her drinking and maybe she would stop to save herself. However, my message went in one ear and out the other. It was during times like this that I wished she would just die so I wouldn't have to deal with her anymore.

Against doctor's warnings, my mother continued to drink. On January 5th, her forty-fifth birthday, her brother Bobby died of a drug overdose. At this point in our relationship, I was barely speaking to her, but decided to call her since she no longer lived with my father and me. The phone rang and she answered sobbing, "Hey Mom. It's me, Em. I just wanted to call and wish you a happy birthday and I'm so sorry about Uncle Bobby. He's in a better, safer place now. I'm so sorry." She just continued to cry and cry, and from what I could hear nothing was going to stop it. "Thanks," she said in a mist of tears then hung up.

With this death, she had finally realized the culmination of all the pain and suffering her life had been. Two of my aunts were coming to stay with my mother for the funeral. That day they kept calling and calling, but no one was answering the phone and it was mid-afternoon. They had a bad feeling in their stomachs that told them something wasn't right. Why wouldn't she answer the phone if she knew they were coming? Once they arrived at my mom's apartment, they slowly stepped out of the car, held each other's hand, and walked to the front door. The door was surprisingly and luckily open. "Tina," they cried out, but no one answered. As they walked in a little further, they approached the couch in the living room to find my mother and the apartment covered in blood.

It was a cold, grey day in the beginning of January 2004. People gathered from around the town of St. Petersburg, Florida for this occasion. It was a gathering of friends and family to commemorate love and celebrate life. It was a funeral. My mother was so loved by the community that the funeral home was busting at the seams with people trailing out into the street. I've never in my life felt so much support from a community of people. My father and I greeted each person that walked in. Each one would hug me tightly and say the same thing, "I am so sorry for your loss," and I would robotically reply, "Thank you." During the service, I looked around me, I looked at my family, and everyone except me was in tears. I couldn't bring myself to cry. I was still so angry and at this point I hated her for what she had done. The person who I always trusted to be there was gone in a blink of an eye. I was paralyzed with shock. I forced myself to cry so that people wouldn't look at me more than they already were. I just wanted it to be over and for things to return to normal, but what was normal? I hadn't known normal for three years.

Six months after her death, I couldn't comprehend what had happened. I blocked out pain and sadness, and anger was the only emotion I felt. I cried because of my anger. I wondered, "How could a mother leave her child? Was I not good enough to save her?" Sadness slowly crept up on me as I began to miss my mother. I sat on my bed and played the messages she left me on my voicemail over and over again just to hear the sound of her voice. I watched old childhood videos to see the happiness and love on both of our faces.

I broke down and finally lost it completely—emotionally, physically, and mentally. However, a bit of hope came my way. While I was being driven to school one day I looked out the window to my right and a blue jay was flying right next to me. At first it freaked me out because I had never seen a bird that close. I remember saying to myself, "You know that was really odd. Maybe if I see it again it will signify that my mom has entered a new life." Sure enough that very same day, I was walking to the bathroom during lunch and a blue jay landed right in front of me and just looked at me. I was shocked, amazed, and so grateful because I knew this was her trying to tell me that everything was all right and that she was in a better place now.

"Please whatever you do don't stop dancing."

I sat in front of my mirror, cross-legged on the floor, looking at myself. The song "Drugs or Me" by Jimmy Eat World played in the background, "If only you could see, the stranger next to me. You promise, you promise that you're done, but I can't tell you from the drugs." Closing my eyes, I started swaying from side to side trying to envision the past three years. All I wanted was clarity. A little swaying cross-legged on the floor, slowly built up to a passionate exploration of my mind, body, and soul. I embodied my mother, the beautiful person I once knew trapped inside a monster. The song played on. "Take me. I need your help, so far to pull me out. Take the wheel, out from me. So far." Leaping, turning, and jumping, I danced vigorously on the hardwood floors of my room. I called out to her through my dancing. I screamed, "I understand. I'm so sorry. I blame you for nothing. I will always love and miss you." The song ends "Always keep me close," as I collapse on the floor, struggling for air, sobbing, yet knowing I had found a way to keep her alive in my heart.

Aftermath

———～ᴗᴗ～———

Piling up tasks was the way I escaped my true feelings about Tina's death. From one day to the next, I felt sadness, anger, anxiety, grief and at times even relief. Emily's nanny, Rebecca, took care of her daily needs and I used a week off from work to stay busy with funeral arrangements and preparing her condo for sale. I had the locks changed and hired a cleaning service to remove the bloodstains from the couch, but ultimately I threw it out—too many memories. Not trusting Billy Barber, I spread out the contents of her wallet and purse on my kitchen table. As I made a dozen phone calls to close her credit and checking accounts, I was amazed at how easy some of it was— name, social security number, and date of birth was all I needed. Some were completely automated.

I stumbled upon several surprises. She had changed her will after the divorce and all of her IRA and other savings were willed evenly to my three daughters. She didn't leave a penny to any of her family. I returned to the condo and walked into her large walk-in clothes closet. As I surveyed the contents, I found two-dozen pairs of jeans, mostly designers, and many with new tags intact. The floor was strewn with purses, old and new, none of them generic or cheap. The hanging racks in her closet seemed liked a whole department of Nordstrom's— blouses, dresses, pants, jackets and sweaters. Coming from poor roots, her addiction to shopping was every bit as real and consuming as was her attachment to alcohol. If she couldn't drink, then she was going to shop—and shop she did. In retrospect, I blamed myself for permitting this to have gone on for so long. I felt weak for not having set reasonable limits for her. What I couldn't give away, a friend with a consignment shop hauled away in two full mini-vans.

I also found in her desk a letter she had written to me but never mailed.

———

I know I've told you this many times before, and therefore you have no reason to believe me. However, I'm so sorry for what I have put you and Emily through. Words can never express how many regrets I have and I'm tired of saying I'm sorry. I'm tired of fighting everything and everybody. If you can find a place in your heart someday, please forgive me.

Love always,
Tina

My initial reaction was anger and sadness—anger at the disease of alcoholism, and sadness at the waste of an otherwise wonderful woman, mother, and wife. I shoved the letter into a bag with other personal items such as sympathy cards and photos. I turned to the task at hand, and needed to make some phone calls. The first one was to the rabbi of my temple. Although I had been on the search committee that had recruited him years ago, he and I never connected. Tina had never converted to Judaism as she had promised before our marriage, and was non-religious. Yet most of our friends and family were Jewish. I picked up the phone on her desk and dialed his number.

"I need to ask you a favor," I said to Rabbi Michael Torop of Temple Beth-El in St. Petersburg, Florida.

"Yes."

"As you know my ex-wife Tina just died and although she was never converted to Judaism and was raised Catholic, she detested that religion. As favor to me and Emily, would you mind officiating at her funeral?"

If he was stunned, he hid it well. His response was immediate and unequivocal.

"No. I don't mind at all."

Jewish law commands that burial be within forty-eight hours of death. Tina had made it quite clear to me that she wanted to be cremated.

"When I die I want to be cremated and spread my ashes off of the dock, like we did for Lucky," she said one day while she visited our marital home on Boca Ciega Bay. Lucky, our medium size beige terrier-mixed breed dog of ten years died shortly after our separation. Tina would die within six months after this conversation.

"I'm okay with the cremation part, but I'm not tossing your ashes off of the dock."

She stared out at the water, eyes reddened and glazed. It was only noon, and she was already hammered.

The day after her death, I visited David Gross, a neighbor and funeral director. I decided to "rent" a wooden coffin from him for the service with an open-casket, and then have her cremated and the remains buried next to her grandmother's grave.

The funeral service was held at the funeral home and not the temple. As family and friends gathered, the number of people overwhelmed me—there was standing room only. As I walked her mother Helen and her natural father, Bruce, up to the casket, I saw him crying for the first time. He would have to bury his son, Bobby later the same day, and then Tina the day after. His large frame and stoical affect were crumbling. Standing at the side of Tina's casket, I remembered what she looked like when she died and what she looked like now. The undertaker had done a very good job of hiding the puffy face and yellowed skin. I had picked out one of her favorite simple dark Betsy Johnson dresses—she finally looked at peace.

I rose to the podium in a dark suit, glanced at my three daughters in the front row, then stared out at the crowded room as the guests began to hush and quiet. I waited until it was completely silent.

"At a time such as this, it would be easy to focus on the tragedy of a young and promising life that ended all too soon. Too easy to speak of the destruction of the love and trust between a husband and wife, and a mother and a daughter by a horrible disease. Instead, I would prefer to share with you the more positive and loving things that I remember about Tina—things such as a warm and caring wife, mother, and an outstanding cook, who could only be matched in the kitchen by her loving husband's penchant and talents for gourmet recipes. In fact, when we would entertain, it would always be in the kitchen, as we would breeze through a dinner preparation as our guests watched, in what Tina would refer to as a 'finely tuned machine.' Or the first time she bought me flowers, and I had to admit that no woman had ever done that for me before. Or when we were in New Orleans once, on the River Walk, having chicory coffee and beignets, and walked past a Victoria's Secret. I asked her what it was, and she laughed, saying 'You don't know what Victoria's Secret is? Boy, have you ever had a sheltered life!'"

"She had a wonderful sense of humor as well. On one of my birthdays, she and Emily bought me a ceramic coffee cup with a dog imbedded in the center. They filled it for me to the brim, and when I sipped it down to the tiny black nose of the dog, I asked 'Is that a coffee bean?' They both giggled, and as I sipped further and exposed the dogs head, I laughed so loud and deep that coffee spewed out of my nose, and we all laughed until we began to cry."

"She forced me to find a hobby; and with her pushing, I ended up with a love affair with fishing—an affair that led me to buy a home on the water and now a way too expensive fishing boat. She was always so generous that every panhandler got at least one dollar from her. Tina loved children, and her many nieces and nephews were her endless delight. However, the light of her life was that gorgeous baby, now beautiful young woman, she bore with the still very red hair— Emily. She gave freely of her time and money to those in need, such as CASA for battered women, Resurrection House for the homeless, and Academy Prep—the magnet school for gifted but disadvantaged inner city youth. She loved and supported the arts, particularly dance and local theater. She would laugh and tease me about my business acumen, and the fact that I could never balance a checkbook, while she could nail it down to the last dime!"

"It has been said that there are only two human emotions. One is love and the other is fear. All other emotions grow out of these two. Fear begets anger and anger begets resentment. Tina, like most of us, lived her life in and out of both of those emotions, but ultimately succumbed to a disease based only on fear. No amount of nagging, pleading, cajoling, bribing, or begging or bargaining can bend or break the disease of addiction. It is a evil disease that knows nothing else other than to sap every fiber of love from its victims, and their families. It is an emotional parasite. Only unconditional love and faith in God, or a higher power, can defeat this monster. The victim is trapped in a web of misery, self-hate and denial."

"I would ask that you all remember her only in the world of love, and not the one of fears. Furthermore, as a true memorial to her memory, the greatest gift you could possibly give to her is to love one another. This family has too long suffered from fear, and anger, and hurt. It is time to let those useless and destructive emotions go. It is time to start healing. And true healing can grow only from unconditional love and forgiveness. We do not need to like one another as a family, but we do need to love one another."

"Please let go all your resentments today. Resentment is like a poison that you swallow, and then wait for the person you are resenting to die! Please cast off any regrets as well. Regret is a useless emotion.

It is a waste of energy; you can't build on it, it's only good for wallowing in. If you can learn nothing else from this past week's tragic deaths of both Tina and her brother Bobby, let it be that there will no longer be room in your hearts for fear, anger, and resentment. I think that would be the greatest gift you all could give one another in her memory. There is no need for you or your children and loved ones to suffer anymore. Forgiving is not forgetting, it's letting go of the hurt."

The final words came out as I choked back my tears. Rachel and Sarah had asked if they could say a few words as well. I didn't ask them to read me what they were going to say. I trusted it would be appropriate and fitting. It would be their final good-byes as well. Rachel spoke first.

"Last night Emily and I were doing facials, when she asked me, 'Did you like my mom at first?'"

I told her, 'Yes, of course.' In fact, Sarah and I adored Tina from the first moment we met her. Tina was a charmer, warm and inviting. We spent many girl nights giving each other facials, back rubs, and learning how to braid hair. You could say we came to quickly love Tina as part of the family."

Sarah spoke next.

"I can remember, when my father and Tina broke up briefly in the beginning of their relationship—Rachel and I were devastated. We even went so far to create a Styrofoam car with a picture of Tina's face inside with another man. We shoved the car into our father's face and said, 'Daddy, this is what will happen if you don't get back together with Tina.' As you can see, Rachel and I were so attached to Tina that the thought of her not being in our lives upset us."

Rachel: "Tina was not just a second mother figure to us—she was our friend and someone who we could always talk to and know that she was more than willing to listen. We thank God for blessing us with her presence in our lives—no matter how brief. We take solace in the fact that things in life happen for a reason no matter how hard or difficult they may seem."

Sarah: "Some people come into our lives and quickly go. Some people stay for a while longer and give us a deeper understanding of what is truly important in this life. They touch our souls—we gain strength from the footprints they have left on our hearts and we will never be the same. Tina we love you for the wonderful person you were and we will always keep a special place for you in our hearts."

Rachel: "May God bless you and keep you. We love you always."

The rest of the service was a blur. However, the burial of her ashes was not. They were finally laid to rest in a plain brass box in the same plot as her grandmother on a bright and sunny January day, underneath a large southern oak tree with massive gnarled roots and dripping with tendrils of Spanish Moss. The attendance was much smaller than that of the memorial service the previous day and I knew that was what she would have always wanted; to finally join in the everlasting with her grandmother—the only person to raise her like a real mother, a friend, who tried in vain to save her from the evil that was Victor Morgan. He had been at the memorial service the day before, and was there at the graveside with Helen. He must have slipped away from his wife as the urn was being lowered into the grave. As a perverted footnote, I caught him out of the corner of my eye, taking pictures of the internment. Why, I had no idea—I had never seen anyone do that before, and others later noted the oddity of it as well. Like other bizarre sidebars in her bittersweet life, I let it pass without further comment. I did however make a mental note to do everything in my power to keep him out of my daughter's life forever. I knew that Tina would have wanted it that way.

As the days and weeks sailed by, I experienced a roller coaster of emotions. My anger dissipated, and slowly, the memories became loving and fond. I would find old photos and notes, and saved most. I knew that finally Tina had found that peace which she so desperately sought, yet had always eluded her. There is a saying in Alcoholics Anonymous that no alcoholic dies for naught. If her death could save even one other person's life from the horror of this disease, then perhaps this indeed was God's plan.

Emily was twelve when her mother died. Ironically, about the same age as when Tina's abuse had begun—a very fragile time in any young girl's life, to be sure. She tried hard to not show any emotions during either service. She would later tell me she knew people expected to see her cry—she just couldn't. To this day, she continues to struggle with not having fully grieved for her mother. I made it my task to break the cycle of fear, anger and shame, by showing her unconditional love as the alternative. As for me, there was now, and would always be one new goal—to live my life full of acceptance, love, and gratitude.

Afterword

We were ordering breakfast at the 3rd Street Café in Boca Grande, Florida on Saturday, January 15, 2011. My wife and I had left St. Pete to spend the weekend there on the tip of Gasparilla Island, at the mouth of Charlotte Harbor, well known for two things: tarpon fishing and Hurricane Charley in 2004. I had promised her I would leave my mobile phone at the hotel, but having a premonition, had taken it anyway. It rang and I noticed Pam's name on the caller ID. Denise frowned.

"I'm going to throw that thing in the ocean," she said.

Ignoring the comment for the moment, I glanced at the caller identification. Seeing that it was Pam, I decided to answer it.

"Vic died early this morning," she said.

"How?" I answered, taken off guard.

"He had fluid in his lungs, and they took him to St. Anthony's Hospital. I guess he died in the emergency room."

"Does Helen know?" I asked.

"Not yet," she answered. "You know she's in her own world now," referring to her dementia and rehab from a recent stroke.

"I can't talk now but I will call you later," I said and hung up.

"What's up?" Denise said to me, still miffed.

"Vic died," I said.

She wanted to know the details and of course I had none.

Justice had not been served, but for the abused children, there was a complex of emotions. In speaking with them later, the common answer was, "I don't know how I feel."

Nor did I. Thoughts raced through my mind about calling each sister and asking them for final reflections. However, advice from my wife convinced me otherwise.

We were walking around Miller's Marina, looking at boats, as I tried to keep my mind busy with other thoughts. Looking at the construction of a new "high and dry" metal boathouse for storing boats, I spoke with the dock master. He was a tall gruff Old Florida fishing type—hands worn from cuts and bruises, smell of tobacco, and a baseball cap which said "Penn" for the fishing rod and reel manufacturer.

"Did the storm take out the old one?" I asked.

"Yes," he answered.

Knowing that the landfall had been just a few miles from here, the small but powerful Category Four storm had winds just shy of 160 mph, which would have made it a Category Five like Hurricane Andrew or Katrina, both with devastating results.

He continued. "A local fisherman here had an anemometer on his roof. It stopped working when the wind speed clocked 150 mph."

I nodded my head, knowing all too well firsthand the power of these storms. I had been in Mobile, Alabama in 1979, when Hurricane Frederick hit and my family had no power for nine days.

Glancing at the still waters and mangrove trees, Denise was frank with me.

"You've written two books about her, it's been seven years now. When are you going to let it go?" she said to me.

At first I was defensive. However, upon reflecting further, I knew I had to finally close this chapter in my life.

"You're right," I said. "I need to get past this."

I then began a slow detachment from the Ackerson family and all of its drama. Vic would be cremated, his ashes spread who knows where. A short obituary appeared in the January 20, 2011 edition of the St. Petersburg Times. As I read it I felt nothing—not anger, sadness, or even relief. The only emotion was emptiness.

MORGAN, VICTOR L

78, of St. Petersburg, passed away January 15, 2011. He was employed at the St. Petersburg Times in News. Survivors include his wife Helen, brother Richard of Michigan; and his stepchildren, Pam Barden of Ft. Myers, Bruce Ackerson of Minnesota, Chip Ackerson of Melbourne Beach, Sue Callahan of Dunnellon, Janey Tribou of St. Petersburg, Meighan Jenks of Georgia, and Penny Weinger of Hollywood. (I deleted the one brother's name at his request.)

Conspicuously absent was Jodi's name, which I assume she asked her sisters, who wrote the obituary, not to include. Missing also were either of Vic's sons, from his first marriage, who he had lost custody from years ago, was forbidden to visit, and stayed forever estranged. It was rumored that he had sexually abused them as well and hence another missing piece of the puzzle, and failed justice, that was Victor Morgan.

No funeral service was held. Over the objections of several of her sisters, Sue would later tell me that about a week after his death, she finally told Helen during a moment of her mother's lucidity. Sue's only description was "she took it well."

Part of me of course wanted more interviews, more details, and more answers. But this time I took the advice of my wife—this had to end. To do otherwise, would commit me to an endless road of investigation and questions which I chose no longer to pursue.

"You're right," I said to Denise. "This is our anniversary."

"Thank you," she said.

"So where do you want to go for dinner?" I asked.

She smiled and said, "Anywhere. Just as long as it is about us and there are no ghosts at the table."

I nodded in agreement. And as we would later dine, our waitress asked us if this was a special occasion.

"Yes," I said. "It is our fifth wedding anniversary."

"Would you like a bottle of wine or champagne to celebrate?" she asked, handing me a wine list.

For the briefest of moments, I reflected back on a deceased wife, and a former life that now seemed light years away, and then answered.

"No thanks. I think we'll just stick with the water."

CPSIA information can be obtained at www.ICGtesting.com
Printed in the USA
LVOW06s0031180314

377782LV00011B/202/P